AF148391

RMS AQUITANIA

THE SHIP BEAUTIFUL

SOUVENIR OF
THE LAUNCHING
OF
R·M·S·AQUITANIA
APRIL · 1913

CUNARD·STEAM·SHIP·CO·LTD

An ornate piece of artwork.
(Mike Poirier collection)

RMS AQUITANIA

THE SHIP BEAUTIFUL

MARK CHIRNSIDE

The History Press

First published 2008
Reprinted 2009, 2022, 2026

The History Press
97 St George's Place,
Cheltenham, Gloucestershire, GL50 3QB
www.thehistorypress.co.uk

© Mark Chirnside, 2008

The right of Mark Chirnside to be identified as the Author of this work has been
asserted in accordance with the Copyrights, Designs and Patents Act 1988.

All rights reserved. No part of this book may be reprinted or reproduced or utilised in
any form or by any electronic, mechanical or other means, now known or hereafter
invented, including photocopying and recording, or in any information storage or
retrieval system, without the permission in writing from the Publishers.

British Library Cataloguing in Publication Data.
A catalogue record for this book is available from the British Library.

ISBN 978 0 7524 4444 4

Typesetting and origination by The History Press
Printed by Imak, Turkey

EU Authorised Representative: Easy Access System Europe
Mustamäe tee 50, 10621 Tallinn, Estonia
gpst.request@easproject.com

For Sue, and for everyone who has encouraged my research.

'No ship in modern maritime history has had a more honourable and
distinguished record. She was one of the queens of the transatlantic fleet. She
was, in two wars, a troopship, an armed merchant carrier, a hospital ship, a
great transport, a ferry for war brides, and, finally, a ship of hope for displaced
persons.

But to those in New York she was something else. She was a recurrent
adornment to the waterfront skyline. Her famous four stacks were there after
her sister ships disappeared. She was unmistakable; dignified, proud, often
sedate, always the great lady. Those who travelled on her know of her comfort;
those who watched her know of her beauty. She was a great and a proud ship…'
– The *New York Times*, 17 December 1949.

CONTENTS

ACKNOWLEDGEMENTS

As always, this project has been a team effort. I have renewed many friendships as I researched and wrote this book, and formed new ones. There's a debt of gratitude that I owe to many people who were kind and generous in terms of sharing material, contributing ideas and offering encouragement. As always, any mistakes are my fault alone.

I would like to thank my parents, Ghislaine and David, family and friends, for their ongoing encouragement with my writing. My thanks are due to many institutions and archives, including the helpful staff of the Cunard Archives at Liverpool University's Sydney Jones Library; the staff of the Maritime Archives and Library at Merseyside Maritime Museum; the Public Records Office (now the National Archives) in London; and the Maritime Museum of the Atlantic in Halifax.

Special Collections Librarian Alison Cullingford of Bradford University's J.B. Priestley Archive; Collections Manager (Image Archives and Reproduction Service) Maggie Arbour-Doucette and the staff of the Canadian War Museum; Archives Technician George Gardner of the Glasgow University Archive Services; and Archivist Anthony Richards and the staff of the Imperial War Museum.

My sincere thanks for allowing me to quote material go to the copyright holders of the papers of: Writer John William 'Jack' Clay – Dr Ian Clay; Mrs Penny T. Martin – Mr P.E.N. Martin; Regimental Quarter Master Sergeant Edward Miles – Mrs R. Maytum; Private G. A. Handford – Mr M.G. Reene of the Royal British Legion (on behalf of the late Mrs Barbara N. Parnell). As per my usual practice, the references to these documents at the Imperial War Museum are given directly by endnote, rather than in the primary source section of the bibliography. I regret that, despite all efforts, it has been impossible to contact the copyright holders of the papers of Lieutenant Harold Blake and Private Ernest Lye. Thanks are due to the PFD agency, acting on behalf of the estate of J.B. Priestley, who granted kind permission to quote extracts from his text.

Steve Anderson's correspondence and insights; Günter Bäbler for his research assistance and translation; Clyde George's great enthusiasm and encouragement; Roger Griffiths' valued corrections; Remco Hillen for his generosity; Brent Holt for sharing research materials, assisting with captioning, and some enjoyable discussions; Daniel Klistorner for his encouragement and assistance; Oliver Lörscher for his important input; Michael Lowrey's valuable contributions; Michail Michailakis for his ongoing support and photographic assistance; Mike Poirier for sharing some fascinating information; Hilary Thomas for her considerable patience and research assistance.

For supplying illustrative material, my thanks are due to Ian Boyle; Darren Clossin; Clyde George; Brian Hawley; Jim Kalafus; Daniel Klistorner; J. Kent Layton; Richard Lillard; Eric K. Longo, whose restoration of the many colour slides is remarkable; Chris Mazzella; Chris McBrien; Janette McCutcheon; Michael Pocock; Mike Poirier; Joseph Spletzer; Richard Weiss, for his extensive assistance and restoration work. His generosity in sharing such fine colour images is a shining example of his kindness. Although every effort has been made to trace copyright holders, in the event that any oversights have occurred these can be corrected willingly in any future editions.

I appreciate Scott Andrews' assistance and expertise; Brian Hawley and Eric Sauder for supplying and scanning the gorgeous colour plans, which added considerably to the book at a late stage; while Eric K. Longo put me in touch with John Maxtone-Graham and Norman Morse, whose generous assistance saved me from a statistical error.

And, last but not least, my grateful thanks to my editor, Amy Rigg, and everyone at The History Press – Sophie Atkins, Jack Fulford, Jennifer Lawson, Tom Milner and Emily Locke – for finally making this book a reality.

INTRODUCTION

*A*quitania led a long and eventful life. I first encountered the legendary Cunarder's history when I was researching the White Star Line's Olympic-class liners: *Olympic* (launched 1910), *Titanic* (1911) and *Britannic* (1914). Conceived in part as Cunard's response to the new White Star liners, the company decided to build on the success of *Lusitania* and *Mauretania* by constructing a third liner for their New York express service, which was to be even more luxurious.

For this purpose, Cunard realised that they needed to take their inspiration from other popular liners in service at the time. Their new liner would incorporate some of the best features of the competition, part of a process of continuing improvement. In 1911, *Olympic* was examined and plenty of other liners' features would be incorporated into Cunard's plans. These observations proved useful during the process of designing and building the *Aquitania*. In time Cunard's new ship proved herself a worthy response to the White Star Line, and the Hamburg-Amerika Line's (HAPAG's) trio of 50,000-ton liners: *Imperator* (launched 1912), *Vaterland* (1913) and *Bismarck* (1914). Although fast, the White Star and HAPAG vessels were designed with the emphasis on luxury rather than the supreme speed of *Lusitania* and *Mauretania*.

After a brief spell of passenger service in 1914, *Aquitania* proved herself during the First World War. Following the war, *Aquitania* was a considerable success on the Atlantic passenger run in the 1920s and 1930s, providing sterling service in the Second World War as well. She was in service from 1914 to 1950, and that fact alone makes her outstanding. Always one of the most popular liners afloat in her heyday, she was an outstanding success. In 1921, she set a record for the total number of passengers that she carried in a year, a record that none of her rivals were ever able to match.

This concise history of the *Aquitania* is intended to complement previous histories, by focusing on rare and previously unpublished information drawn from a variety of sources. It is in the photographs and illustrations that this book's greatest strength lies, and I would like to thank everyone who shared material. It is such a gorgeous collection of rare, and visually stunning, images that have made this book what it is.

Mark Chirnside
May 2008

one

INTO THE TWENTIETH CENTURY

Although Cunard's *Lusitania* and *Mauretania* proved an immense success as the fastest liners in the world, there was no time for rest. The company could not afford to ignore their rivals as they built liners of ever-increasing comfort and luxury.

Any running mate would need to be capable of maintaining a speed that withstood critical comparison. Years later, a Cunard lecturer recalled:

> ... in regard to speed, two chief points had to be considered. The ship would have to leave either terminal port, Liverpool or New York, once every three weeks and, to avoid an expensively rapid 'turn around' in port, not more than 5½ days could be allowed for the voyage. A speed of 23 knots was therefore decided upon.

As well as the timetabling requirements, the ship's form had to be considered: 'She was to be a sea-hotel, a fast, safe and steady sea boat. She was not to be too big, too long or too deep to enter existing harbours on either side of the Atlantic.' She also needed to pay her way. On 17 March 1910 several plans were submitted to the company's board for a 'new fast steamer' with a service speed of 23 knots, to be powered by steam turbines.

One letter, dated two days earlier, specified that any proposed design for the new ship must not 'have less metacentric height than obtained on the *Lusitania* and *Mauretania*.' As a method of measuring a ship's stability, the new liner's metacentric height would be an important means of ensuring that she was steady and comfortable when at sea. Several proposals were outlined. Plan A was for a ship 775ft long, with a breadth of 91ft and a moulded depth of 62ft 6in – slightly shorter than the *Mauretania* and a little wider. The general arrangement would comprise an open promenade, first-class public rooms and staterooms on A-deck; a covered promenade and staterooms on B-deck; a complete deck of staterooms on C-deck; dining saloons on D-deck; a working passageway for the crew, with galleys and crew areas on E-deck; and third-class passenger accommodation and stores on F- and G-decks. Plan B specified a ship with the same number of decks as the *Mauretania*, with the ship's side plating being carried all the way up to the promenade deck (as opposed to the superstructure) to allow dining saloons to be fitted on the shelter deck. Plan C envisaged space for an additional deck, obtained by reducing the diameter of the boilers and increasing their number, thereby allowing the accommodation decks to be lowered by 3ft. Plan E considered using a three-funnel arrangement as opposed to four funnels. Plan F was merely for a ship with the same number of decks as the *Mauretania*, but without a through passageway underneath the promenade deck. The final plan, G, considered a ship only 760ft long, with a width of 92ft and a moulded depth of 64ft 6in – possessing one more deck than the *Mauretania*.

On 21 July 1910 it was decided that representatives of shipbuilders Messrs Swan, Hunter & Wigham Richardson Ltd, Messrs John Brown & Co. Ltd, and Messrs Vickers Sons & Maxim, would be interviewed and given a preliminary idea of the sort of ship required. By 8 December 1910, John Brown & Co. had been chosen to build the new liner, and seven days later the draft contract was unanimously agreed to by Cunard's board of directors. On 19 January 1911 the name *Aquitania* was approved and seven days later the agreement with the shipbuilders was sealed.

A specification book, dated 28 October 1910, called for the new liner to carry around 660 first-class, 740 second-class and 2,300 third-class passengers, not to mention 830 crew. By the time she was completed, *Aquitania*'s capacities were given as 618 first class, 614 second class, and 1,998 third class, along with 972 crew – no fewer than 4,202 people.[1] The reduction in passenger capacities and increase in the number of crew indicates the improvement throughout

Above: It is interesting to compare *Aquitania*'s profile to that of her running mate, *Lusitania*. *Aquitania* is seen here in Southampton's floating dry dock in the mid-1920s. (J. & C. McCutcheon collection)

Above left: Cunard's *Lusitania* proved an immense success following her entry into service and capture of the Blue Riband in 1907. (J. Kent Layton)

Centre left: *Aquitania* on the stocks in 1913, prior to her launch as the 'latest and largest addition to the Cunard fleet' according to the *New York Times*. Note the incline, with the bow higher than the stern. (J. & C. McCutcheon collection)

Below left: Another view shows the bow's height. While the superstructure is largely in place, the deckhouses are still to be constructed – as is the bridge enclosure. (Clyde George collection)

the design process: 'All the steel used in the structure of the ship [is] to be of the highest quality; all to be of British manufacture', Cunard instructed. They called for the ship's name to be written in 'polished brass' letters at least 18in long. Meanwhile the bridge was 'to be of sufficient height and width to command a good view above the boats and other obstructions fore and aft' of the ship. 'All first class staterooms' were 'to be fitted with an approved wash basin, having a constant supply of hot and cold water.' *Aquitania*'s captain would enjoy a suite of rooms consisting of a 'sitting room, bedroom, bath, and w.c.' The sitting room was to be panelled in 'mahogany, French polished, and to be furnished as an extra first class stateroom'.

Above: Aquitania at Liverpool's landing stage. (Clyde George collection)

Above left: Aquitania leaves the ways… (Clyde George collection)

Left: …and the crowd watch her complete the transition from land to water. (Clyde George collection)

First-class public rooms eventually included a drawing room, two writing salons, a Georgian lounge flanked by two garden lounges, and a smoke room on A-deck, while the first-class foyer (or reception room), Louis XVI restaurant and grill room were placed amidships on D-deck. (Despite the 'restaurant' designation for the first-class dining saloon, it was not an extra-tariff facility, and nor was the smaller grill room, although it provided a more intimate atmosphere.) The main staircase led to a swimming pool and gymnasium below the reception foyer, on E-deck. Second-class passengers had their own lounge, drawing room, smoke room, veranda café, gymnasium and an ample dining saloon. Meanwhile, third class had a large 'non-smoking compartment' (or 'general room') forward on D-deck with its own bar, and a covered promenade beneath it on E-deck, which

also had space for handling baggage. Amidships on E-deck was an even larger third-class area with the same purpose. Aft on D-deck, third class had a large promenade area – open to the sea air – and a covered promenade area beneath it on E-deck. Amidships on F-deck were three third class-dining saloons, from forward to aft seating 332, 286 and 365 passengers.

If the public rooms were impressive, in first class the most expensive accommodation included eight suites on B-deck named after famous painters. Forward of the main staircase on the port side was the Reynolds suite, and on the starboard side the Gainsborough suite. Each included a veranda, sitting room, two bathrooms, a hallway and three ample staterooms. The other six suites varied in size and amenities: amidships on the port side the Romney suite had

THE GRAPHIC, APRIL 12, 1913

⚓ THE ERA OF THE 50,000-TON LINER ⚓
THE STRUGGLE FOR THE SUPREMACY OF THE ATLANTIC

THE RENOVATED OLYMPIC, WHICH LEFT SOUTHAMPTON FOR NEW YORK LAST WEEK ON HER MAIDEN TRIP
In the five months which have elapsed since she was taken out of service, the Olympic has undergone extensive alterations and improvements at a cost of some £300,000, the work including the construction of an inner skin and an increase in the number and height of the water-tight bulkheads. New features have also been added, as shown below, for the comfort of passengers.

THE OLYMPIC'S ENLARGED RESTAURANT

THE OLYMPIC'S READING AND WRITING ROOM

NEW LUXURIES FOR OLYMPIC PASSENGERS
The reception-room in connection with the restaurant.

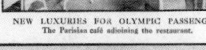

GERMANY'S LARGEST SHIP: THE IMPERATOR
which sails on her maiden trip across the Atlantic next month.

NEW LUXURIES FOR OLYMPIC PASSENGERS
The Parisien café adjoining the restaurant.

GERMANY'S LATEST LEVIATHAN LINER: THE LAUNCH OF THE VATERLAND LAST WEEK AT THE YARD OF BLOHM AND VOSS, HAMBURG
The two new Hamburg-Amerika liners—the Imperator and the Vaterland—may claim to be the largest ships yet afloat, but only until Monday week, when a still larger ship, the Aquitania (illustrated on the following pages) takes the water at Clydebank. The tonnage of each of the German vessels is nearly 50,000, and in luxurious accommodation they will be equal to any of their rivals.

In 1913, *The Graphic* described *Olympic*'s return to service and the advent of *Imperator* and *Vaterland* as 'The Era of the 50,000-ton Liners'. Following the war, *Imperator* became Cunard's *Berengaria* and *Vaterland* the American liner *Leviathan*. (J. & C. McCutcheon collection)

R.M.S. Aquitania.

Postcard illustrations were often used to enhance the profiles of the great liners. In this case, *Aquitania* is depicted, yet the curved forward end of her superstructure and bridge appear like *Lusitania*'s. (Author's collection)

BRITAINS LARGEST LINER LIGHTED THROUGHOUT BY ALL BRITISH
"ROYAL EDISWAN" LAMPS.
T.S.S. "AQUITANIA"   LENGTH 901 FT.   WIDTH 97 FT.   TONNAGE 47,000   SPEED 23 KNOTS.

Although this advert inflated *Aquitania*'s gross tonnage to 47,000 tons (an earlier estimate), Cunard relied on their new liner's length of 901ft to claim that she was 'Britain's largest liner'. (J. & C. McCutcheon collection)

Aquitania's outer propellers were some 86ft forward of the inner propellers, while the ship was 'cut away at the after end for a distance of about 70ft, from the stern, in order to give a clear run of water to the inner propellers. A strong heel casting is fitted at the end of the straight portion of the keel, from which runs the centre girder supporting the propeller brackets and the rudder post…'. The 'cut away' is visible between the inner propellers, ahead of the rudder. (By courtesy of the University of Liverpool Library, Cunard Archives)

Top: Prior to her sea trials, *Aquitania* is seen being coaled in this lovely image. Coaling was a filthy process, as the dust got everywhere, and it was back-breaking work. (Clyde George collection)

Above: *Aquitania*, riding fairly high in the water, is seen here on trials in this lovely 1914 photograph. (J. & C. McCutcheon collection)

a large stateroom, sitting room, veranda and bathroom, while the Raeburn on the starboard side did without a veranda; the Vandyke, Holbein, Velasquez and Rembrandt suites completed the set. Elsewhere on B-deck, there were a number of suites with their own bathrooms, while there were several suites on the port side of C-deck with their own sitting rooms and bathrooms. Almost all first-class staterooms held one or two people, and many of those on B- and C-deck had private bathroom facilities. Second class enjoyed rooms that were spacious for the period, accommodating two, three or sometimes four passengers. As was to be expected, third-class cabins tended to accommodate more passengers, with a number of four- and six-berth rooms, yet aft on F-deck there were a number of rooms accommodating between one and six people which were interchangeable second- and third-class cabins.

While their new liner's design was progressing, Cunard had plenty of reasons to be pleased. In 1911, *Lusitania* completed no fewer than sixteen round trips to New York, carrying 41,377 passengers. Meanwhile, *Mauretania* carried an impressive 38,367 passengers on fourteen round trips. For all their success, Cunard looked to *Aquitania* to complete their intended three-ship express service.

Although they had constructed the *Lusitania*, *Aquitania*'s increased size posed new challenges for the shipbuilder. According to Cunard:

> Several buildings had to be pulled down in order to make room for her, for a berth of over 300 yards in length had to be prepared … Along the entire length of the building slip from the water size inland, massive wooden keel blocks were laid down on which the backbone of the ship was to be put down. Giant cranes on either side were erected in order that the heavy steel plates or frames might be picked up from the mass of accumulated material and placed in any required position.

Aquitania, as built, was larger than early proposals – she was the first Cunarder to exceed 900ft, with an overall length of 901ft 6 in. When she entered service her gross tonnage was calculated at 45,647 tons, rather than the estimate of 47,000 tons that appeared in 1913 publicity material. While *Aquitania* could claim to be longer than *Olympic*, on the basis of gross tonnage she was smaller – *Olympic*'s gross tonnage had increased to 46,358 tons in 1913.

The issue of displacement (essentially a ship's weight) was more complicated. In 1913, *The Shipbuilder* said that with a load draft of 34ft *Aquitania* would displace 49,500 tons;[2] and in the souvenir number of 1914 gave a draft of 36ft and a displacement of 53,000 tons.[3] The higher figure exceeded *Olympic*'s displacement (as her draft of 34ft 7in corresponded to 52,310 tons), yet a 1920 Board of Trade file gave *Aquitania*'s approved draft as 35ft 4in with a displacement of 51,700 tons. By that standard *Olympic*'s displacement was

greater, yet in 1922 *Aquitania*'s approved draft would be increased to 36ft 2in (displacing more than 53,000 tons).[4]

Although gross tonnage can be taken as a better measure of size, both ships had a claim of sorts to being the largest British ship afloat, except for the brief period that White Star's 48,158-ton *Britannic* was in service in 1915–16.

Aquitania's keel had been laid in June 1911, the first step to constructing the hull. The keel was followed by the double bottom and then the framing and plating of the hull itself. The stern frame and propeller brackets weighed no less than 130 tons, while the rudder weighed 70 tons. In just under two years she would be launched. She would embody the experience of operating Cunard's previous steamers, while staff from Lloyd's registry helped determine the necessary structural strength.[5] As for interiors, Cunard wished to engage the design services of Mewès & Davis (of London), yet since Mewès was still under contract to HAPAG it would be Arthur Davis who had 'sole responsibility' for *Aquitania*, while James Miller (famous for designing *Lusitania*'s airy interiors) designed the public rooms.[6]

In October 1912 contracts were being placed and sealed for the ship's interior decoration. Messrs G. Trollope & Son were to decorate the second-class drawing room and the dining room; Messrs Jackson & Sons Ltd were to decorate the second-class lounge and first-class drawing room; Messrs W. & E. Thornton-Smith had the task of completing the first-class smoke room; and Messrs Turpin & Co. were given the task of decorating the swimming bath, gymnasium, and the related vestibule and corridor. Six days later, Messrs Wylie & Lochhead Ltd won the contract for the decoration of the first-class grill room and vestibule.

Aquitania's launch date was set for 21 April 1913. At the time, *Aquitania* weighed no less than 22,000 tons, and eight sets of chains weighing a total of 1,400 tons were required to bring the ship to a halt after she had been launched by the Countess of Derby. From that point, several tugs were required to tow the ship to the fitting-out berth, where the interiors would be completed and she would be transformed from a steel shell into an elegant floating town. No time was lost in explaining that 'miles of electric wires were being laid along seemingly endless corridors', nor that thousands of skilled workers were involved in the ship's fitting-out – from plumbers to plasterers, and carvers to carpet fitters. Later in *Aquitania*'s career, Cunard said that the ship's electrical equipment was powerful enough to 'light a town of 100,000 inhabitants'. Two hundred miles of cable were used, not to mention 700 miles of wires weighing no less than 45 tons. These powered almost 10,000 lights and 1,500 bell pushes throughout the ship, while the kitchens alone contained forty different types of electrical appliances.[7]

Cunard were keen to emphasize their new liner's safety, little more than a year after the loss of the *Titanic*. The company indicated that they had always planned there would be 'lifeboats for all', and this seems entirely plausible since

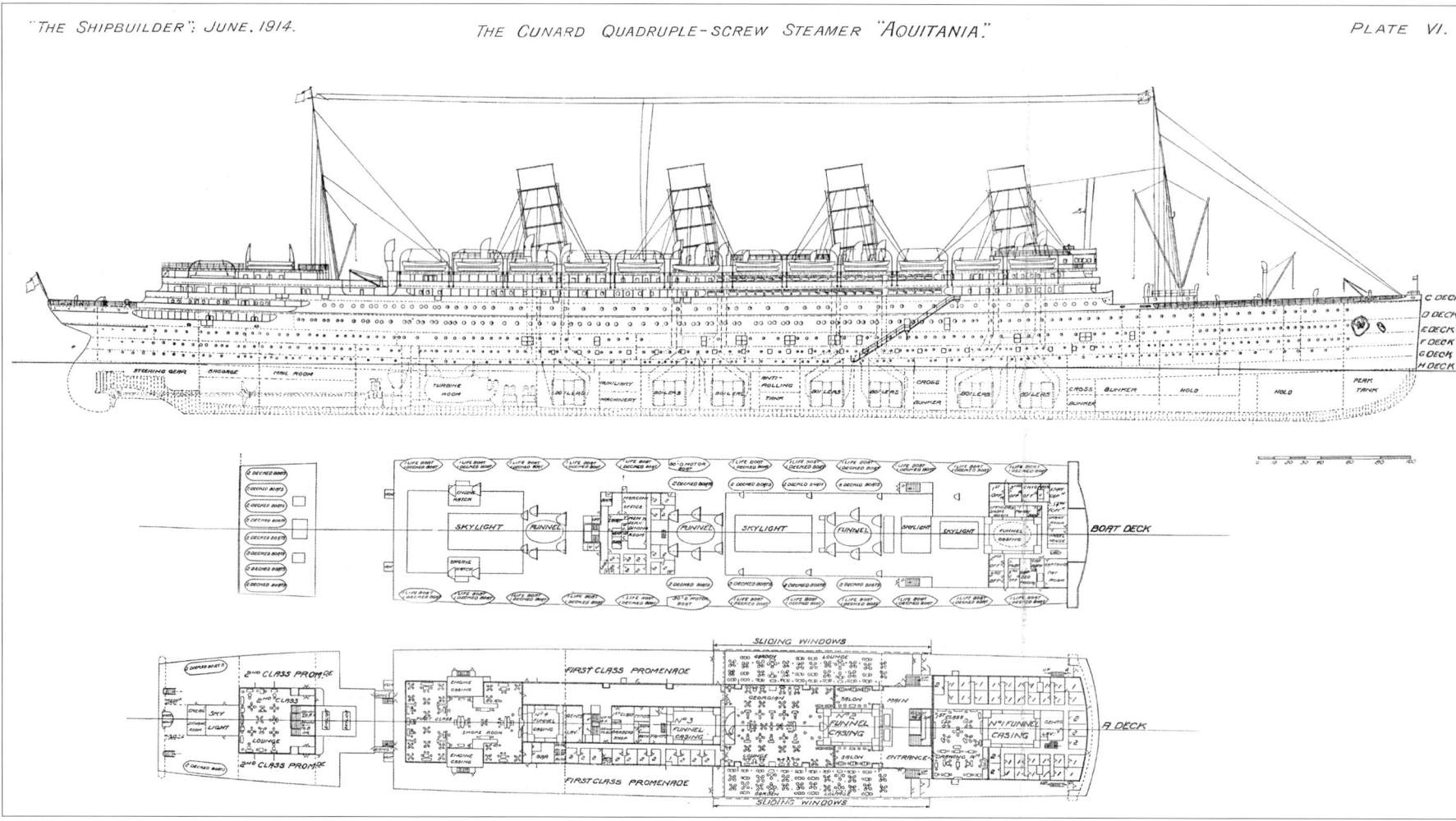

"THE SHIPBUILDER": JUNE, 1914.   THE CUNARD QUADRUPLE-SCREW STEAMER "AQUITANIA".   PLATE VI.

Above and opposite: The Shipbuilder, a respected shipping journal, issued full descriptions of *Aquitania* in June 1914. This side elevation and deck plans can be compared to the 1938 accommodation plan (seen on page 68). (J. & C. McCutcheon collection)

Chairman Alfred Booth had written to the Board of Trade's Sir Walter Howell on 18 May 1912:

> I do not myself believe that there is any possible half-way house between the present Board of Trade Rules and the supply of boats or rafts for every soul on board. As you know, I had already come to this conclusion in considering what we should have to do for the *Aquitania* as long ago as February last.

Publicity material called her 'a ship within a ship', and 'the division of the ship into watertight compartments is much more extensive than is required by any regulations', Cunard told the press. As *The Shipbuilder* recorded:

> …The double bottom is divided into more than forty separate compartments. An important feature of the *Aquitania*, as in the *Lusitania* and *Mauretania*, is that for quite one-half of the ship's length longitudinal bulkheads are provided at an average distance of about fifteen feet from the outer skin plating, thus forming

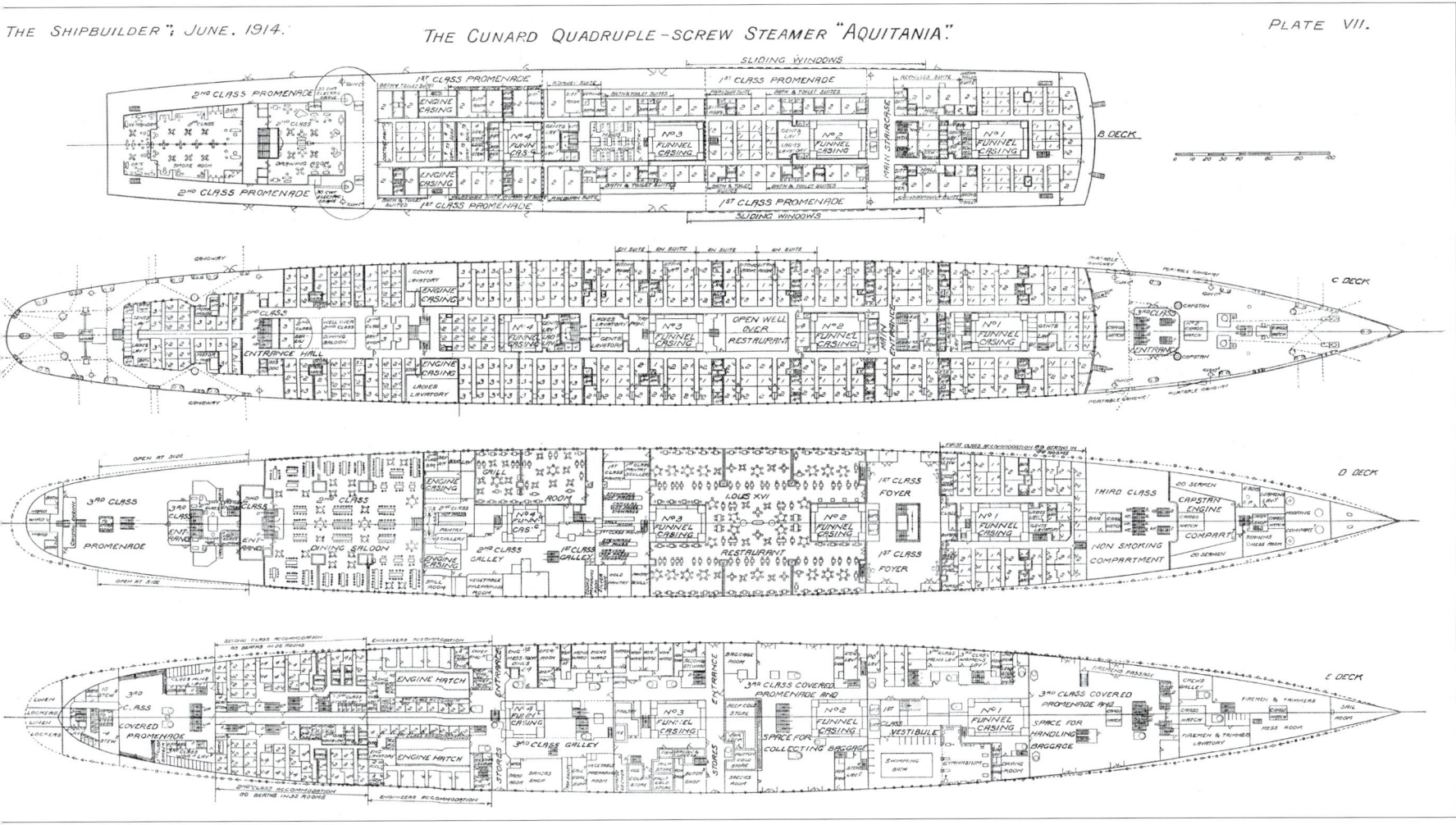

THE SHIPBUILDER; June. 1914.   THE CUNARD QUADRUPLE-SCREW STEAMER "AQUITANIA".   PLATE VII.

what may be termed 'a ship within a ship'. The intervening spaces between the longitudinal bulkheads and the ship's sides are divided by bulkheads at short intervals into relatively small cellular compartments. In addition, there are sixteen transverse watertight bulkheads extending right across the vessel, the majority of which are carried to at least nineteen feet above the waterline, while in no case do they terminate less than ten feet above the waterline. As a further provision for safety, two decks are made watertight, all the openings cut in these decks being trunked up to the top of the sheer with watertight trunks. The bulkhead doors in the lower part of the ship are operated by hydraulic power on the Stone-Lloyd system, in which, by a movement of a lever on the bridge, the navigating officer can close all the doors simultaneously should the necessity arise for doing so.

The Shipbuilder published flooding curve diagrams, showing the ship floating with five large watertight compartments flooded aft, G-deck's watertight integrity intact as designed but H-deck damaged. *Aquitania*'s draft forward was only 22ft 7in, yet at the stern she drew 60ft 5in, with the waterline up to D-deck and the counter submerged. Mark Warren praises the ship's subdivision that, 'theoretically, would allow the first five consecutive compartments forward, or the last five compartments aft, to be flooded

S.S. Aquitania,
Sailing down the Clyde,
Sunday 10th May, 1914.

Top left: This aged card has a wonderful atmospheric quality. (Author's collection)

Above left: Aquitania in the Gladstone Dock prior to her maiden voyage in May 1914. (J. & C. McCutcheon collection)

Left: Aquitania was coaled with the assistance of Scott's Coaling Gear. (*The Shipbuilder*, 1914/ author's collection)

Top right: Aquitania's bulk is impressive, seen here at Liverpool before her maiden voyage. The white notice on the starboard side of the stern rail warns people to 'keep clear of propellers'. (Clyde George collection)

Above right: Aquitania leaves Liverpool, in a wonderful image apparently dating from her maiden departure, 30 May 1914. (Clyde George collection)

without sinking the ship, provided all portholes were closed. If there were damage amidships, the nine watertight longitudinal coal bunkers lining the port or starboard sides of the four boiler rooms, and the wing engine and condenser compartments could also be flooded without seriously endangering the ship.'[8]

Yet, despite the grand scheme of things, Cunard were keen to ensure that the smaller luxuries were not overlooked and continued to modify proposals for the new liner's lavish interiors. On 5 July 1913, Cunard proposed that the first-class grill room's ceiling remain a plain design, since an 'ornamental plaster ceiling should not be put in, as it will make the room

As she comes into New York for the first time, *Aquitania*'s paintwork on the bow is the worse for wear – a common sight, also evident on photos of *Olympic*'s maiden arrival. After several coats of black paint, it was no longer so obvious when the top coat wore away. (Clyde George collection)

At Fishguard on the return leg of the maiden voyage, *Aquitania* appears to be listing to starboard. *Shipbuilding & Shipping Record* commented on 18 June 1914 that she was: '...a finished ship and one worthy of the title she earned from the passengers as "The Ship Beautiful". There is indeed an elegant simplicity about the scheme of decoration which imparts an air of restfulness and quietude onboard and which renders the ship as impressive when viewed from within as the graceful lines of her hull did when she majestically entered Fishguard Harbour with the rising sun.' (Clyde George collection)

too much like the *Olympic*'s [first-class] dining saloon.' Similarly, 'double windows should not be reintroduced into this room.' In the event, with the Jacobean style it hardly looked dissimilar to her White Star rival. By early October 1913 there were concerns about the progress being made with the interior decoration. A memo to Cunard's general manager stated that 'the workmanship continues to be satisfactory, but the rate of progress is slow.' The second-class drawing room and smoke room, and first-class D-deck staterooms were cited as problems: 'None of the places are in a sufficiently advanced state to allow of the firms to proceed with their work.' Things were soon looking up again. On 28 January 1914, work on the main first-class staircase, and the first- and second-class dining rooms had been begun 'and very fair progress' had been made. Meanwhile, the first class grill room was 'practically completed.' Work had begun on decorating the first-class drawing room, but the first-class smoke room, second-class lounge, drawing room and smoke room were still 'in a very backward condition.'

There was also concern over rising costs. Cunard had laid down a price of £3,000 to decorate the first-class writing room, but the contractor's estimate had reached £5,000; and the first-class lounge decoration was estimated to cost £5,457, yet Cunard's budget had set aside only £4,000. Including furniture, the lounge cost £9,675 as the estimate was amended to £5,546.[9] Cunard requested changes to reduce costs. Proportionately, more money was spent on *Aquitania*'s first-class furnishings than on the décor itself – reversing what had happened on *Mauretania* – as tastes moved to simpler, yet nevertheless stylish, décor.[10] There were the inevitable minor difficulties in outfitting such a large liner, yet twelve months after her launching, *Aquitania* was complete.

Cunard had reason to be pleased, as in a matter of weeks *The Shipbuilder* would write: 'the excellent results achieved are unsurpassed in any vessel afloat, either in general utility or beauty of decoration.'[11] The journal was not prone to giving bad reviews, yet it definitely had a point when it praised the large proportion of single berth staterooms in first class, noting that 'wooden bedsteads almost entirely replace the traditional "bunk".'[12] They appeared more like hotel rooms. 98 per cent of *Aquitania*'s first-class rooms were single or double berths, compared to 61 per cent on *Olympic*. The *Shipbuilder* commented on the 'unusually spacious' second-class promenades, while praising the veranda café as 'new' to second class.[13] *Aquitania* reflected previous innovations: her enclosed promenade decks were similar to *Titanic*'s; her first-class dining saloon floor plan was 'very similar' to *Olympic*'s, though the décor owed more to *Amerika*;[14] her second-class café aft was similar to *Lusitania*'s first-class café; and her first-class main staircase bore resemblance to both *Imperator*'s and *Lusitania*'s. *Aquitania*'s long gallery was partially inspired by the corridor aft of *Olympic*'s first-class lounge, which was comparably far smaller than the gallery on the Cunarder. Cunard decided not to install a Turkish bath (unlike the German and White Star ships), or an indoor squash court, yet *Aquitania*'s interiors were a winning combination. As her sea trials approached, all eyes were on the new liner.

NOTES

1 *Shipbuilder* 2, page 211.

2 *Shipbuilder* 2, page 195.

3 *Shipbuilder* Special Number, page 34.

4 The increase, following *Aquitania*'s post-war conversion to oil fuel, was 'required to permit loading with sufficient oil fuel to make a round voyage'.

5 *Shipbuilder* 2, op. cit.

6 *Aquitania*, pages 21–22.

7 *Engineering* Special, page v.

8 The *New York Times* reported after the launch that 'it is expected that the *Aquitania* will be the swiftest liner in the world, half a knot an hour faster than the German [HAPAG] vessels and faster even than the *Lusitania* and the *Mauretania*.' Exaggeration of the express liners' attributes was rife during this period.

9 *Engineering* Special, page vii.

10 *Engineering* Special, op. cit.

11 *Shipbuilder* Special Number, page 114.

12 *Shipbuilder* op. cit., page 125.

13 *Shipbuilder* op. cit., pages 131 and 13.

14 *Engineering* Special, page vi

two

BUILDING THE FUTURE

*A*quitania left the builder's yard on 10 May 1914, steaming from Clydebank to the Tail of the Bank in three hours – a leisurely pace for the twenty-mile distance.[1] More than 2,000 tons of coal was on board, not to mention enough ballast to ensure that she would perform as might be expected in actual service on the Atlantic. The trials began two days later, and *The Shipbuilder* described:

> The turbines were gradually worked up to full power, and runs were made over the measured mile at Skelmorlie at progressive speeds, beginning at 12 knots. Following these runs, high power and full power tests were run between Holy Isle and Ailsa Craig, when speeds of 24 knots were reached with ease, and this notwithstanding the fact that the vessel had not been docked between the date of her launch and the commencement of the trials.[2]

All in all, the new liner exceeded expectations, and hopes were high when *Aquitania* arrived in the Mersey on 14 May 1914, entering the Gladstone dock for hull cleaning the next day.[3] On 29 May 1914, she left the dock in preparation for the maiden voyage. It was reported that 1,000 guests were entertained on-board ship, while 1,055 passengers would be enjoying the maiden voyage. Leaving Liverpool on the afternoon of 30 May 1914, finishing touches were still being added by workmen even as the maiden voyage began. However, with the *Empress of Ireland* disaster, a wireless message reported:

> For the first few hours out of Liverpool it was painfully apparent that the nerves of some passengers were overstrung by reading the harrowing accounts of the loss of the *Empress of Ireland*… In a short space of time environment triumphed. Everything aboard this biggest British liner afloat was so suggestive of a first

class hotel and fashionable life ashore that the passengers quite forgot the perils conjured by the cables from Rimouski.

> It speaks well for the Cunard Line and also for the common sense of the average transatlantic voyager that not a single passage was cancelled on account of the Canadian disaster. The *Aquitania* is proving herself a steady ship and easily managed.

National pride was at stake, with Germany's *Vaterland* fresh into service. Among her features were the split funnel uptakes, which allowed more spacious public rooms than might otherwise have been the case. One newspaper recorded:

> English experts in naval construction contend that there are disadvantages in the *Vaterland*'s arrangement of funnels, but it remains to be seen whether these are offset by the obvious advantages obtained in the interior construction, permitting the large public rooms on the *Vaterland*. There are no such expansive vistas on the *Aquitania* as on the *Vaterland*, but Englishmen who saw both argue that in compactness and shapeliness the *Aquitania* is superior. They also assert that the *Aquitania*, as a whole, showed greater symmetry of design and decoration.

The first day's run averaged 23.17 knots 'with scarcely a trace of vibration', but according to at least one report she reached a speed of 25 knots. While she passed tramp steamers that rolled heavily in the Atlantic swell, she proved herself 'as stiff as a lighthouse.' At one stage of the crossing *Aquitania* had 'practically stopped for five hours' due to ice and fog, but by 4 June 1914 it was reported that she was 'developing speed that was scarcely expected'. Her highest day's run reached 602 miles, and the *New York Times* stated that, 'the average [speed] so far is better than

Above: The grand first-class entrance. The lift gates were 'of fine wrought iron and glass'. (Author's collection)

Above left: Aquitania's drawing room and library, shown after the war, was situated forward on A-deck's starboard side. (Author's collection)

Centre left: An interesting post-war view of one of *Aquitania*'s salons (or writing rooms) on A-deck. This is the port-side salon, looking ahead to the first-class entrance. Its Louis XVI decoration provided a 'delightful effect', while the grey and gold colours complimented the camel-coloured carpet and Persian rug. (Author's collection)

Below left: The staircase leading to B-deck from the first-class entrance. The panelling was painted French grey, while the Corinthian columns were 'copied from a Louis XVI chateau in France'. (Author's collection)

Opposite, clockwise from top left:

The elegant first-class smoke room.

The ornate first-class 'Palladian' lounge, a room of 'majestic size and proportions'.

One of the popular garden lounges on A-deck.

Aquitania's 'Peacock Alley' (another name for the Long Gallery), connecting the first-class lounge and smoke room on A-deck. (All author's collection)

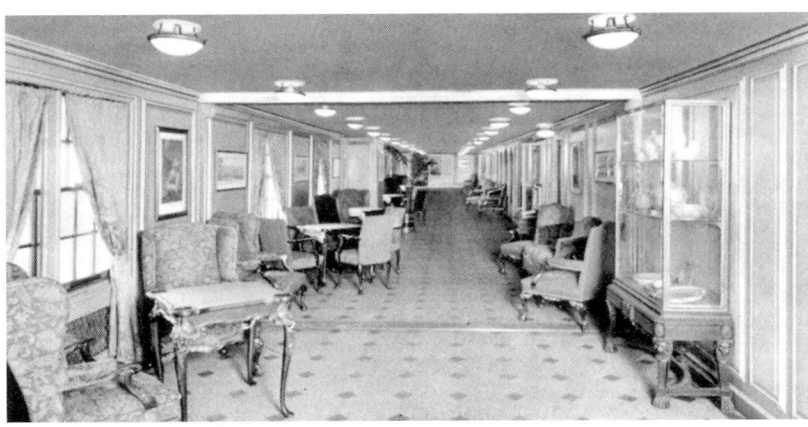

D-deck's spacious first-class foyer, or reception area... (Author's collection)

...which led to the Louis XVI restaurant. (Author's collection)

A lovely image depicting the light elegance of the spacious restaurant. (By courtesy of the University of Liverpool, Cunard Archives)

The Jacobean grill room, 'a more informal and intimate dining room, supplements the main [first-class] restaurant.' (Author's collection)

The first-class gymnasium. (Author's collection)

One of the first-class suite sitting rooms, showing the elegant interior of the Gainsborough suite. (Author's collection)

Oddly enough, *Aquitania* seems to be listing slightly, judging from the swimming pool. (Author's collection)

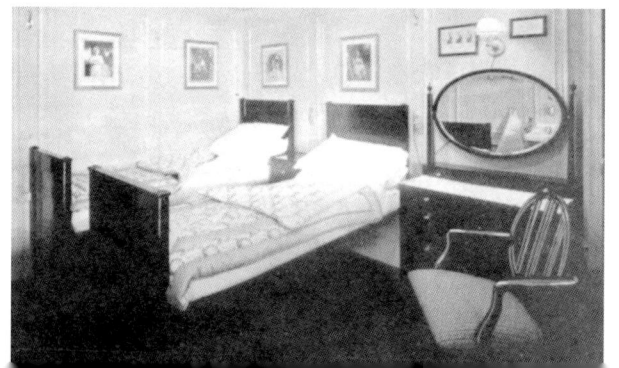

The bedroom of the Romney suite. (Author's collection)

what the *Lusitania* accomplished on her maiden trip.' Captain Turner dispatched a message to Cunard's New York offices:

> Excellent progress so far. Everything is working smoothly. The steadiness and absence of vibration are phenomenal. There is dancing at night as if in harbour. The highest speed in twenty-four hours has been 24.24 knots. The average throughout the voyage has been 23.51 knots.

By the time the *Aquitania* had docked, at 9.35 a.m. on 5 June 1914, it could be reported that she had covered 3,181 miles between Liverpool and the Ambrose Channel Lightship in five days, seventeen hours and forty-three minutes, at an average speed of 23.1 knots. Captain Turner told reporters:

> The average of the run was reduced by having to practically stop for five hours on Tuesday night on account of fog and vicinity of icebergs, but apart from that the weather was grand, and no ship could want a better chance to show what she could do. I do not think the *Aquitania* will ever get better weather than she had this time.

Similar to that of the Reynolds suite, the Romney suite's veranda was cosy. (Author's collection)

Meanwhile, Cunard's Superintendent Engineer John Curry stated that the turbines had 'worked like clockwork' under Chief Engineer Archibald Bryce's direction, while the coal consumption 'was much less than that of the *Mauretania* or *Lusitania*, and the liner had made 24.24 knots for two days during which time she only developed 56,000 horsepower of her 60,000.' Prior to 1907, it would have been a Blue Riband-winning performance!

Yet there were other particularly pleasing aspects for Cunard, when passengers' comments were reported in the New York newspapers. Among them was F. W. Whitridge, president of the Third Avenue Railway, who said that the maiden voyage had been 'the most comfortable trip he had ever made.' *Aquitania* would do well when she departed on the return leg of her maiden voyage, returning (via Fishguard) to Liverpool by 3 p.m. on 16 June 1914. She averaged a swift 23.45 knots. *The Shipbuilder* claimed that *Aquitania* carried 'the largest number of passengers who have ever left New York in a British ship' – no less than 2,649, 'including 675 first class passengers.' Presumably some of the interchangeable rooms had been used to increase first-class capacity.

Cunard were busy monitoring their new ship in the summer of 1914. On 17 June 1914 it was recommended that a mail desk be installed in the first-class drawing room, similar to that onboard the *Lusitania*. *Aquitania*'s main first-class companionway appeared 'to be quite satisfactory and to be quite large enough to cope with the number of passengers and visitors in New York.' Since

One of the single B-deck staterooms. (Author's collection)

'Probably the largest second-class dining saloon on the ocean…' *Aquitania*'s passengers enjoyed the choice of 'smaller tables for groups of four and eight'. (Author's collection)

The elegant drawing room for second-class passengers. (Author's collection)

Another view of the spacious saloon. (Author's collection)

Large windows allowed in a great deal of light. (Author's collection)

the staircase was so wide, a handrail needed to be installed, although there was a more serious problem with the two passenger elevators which 'did not work quite as smoothly as could have been desired'. In particular, the elevator gates needed adjustment as they were noisy. The linoleum joints in the first-class salons, much used by passengers for writing letters, had opened up and needed to be relaid. On several occasions, the first-class lounge had been crowded but the ventilation appeared satisfactory, one problem being that the dance floor was not quite large enough. Passengers had particularly enjoyed the dances in the garden lounges, and it was suggested that the dance floor in the middle of the lounge might be used for dancing in the winter,

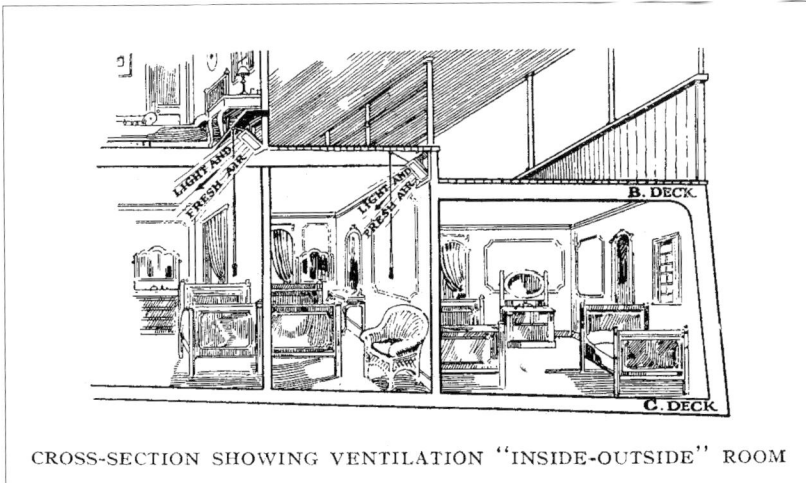

CROSS-SECTION SHOWING VENTILATION "INSIDE-OUTSIDE" ROOM

Illustrating the benefits of the raised section of the promenade on B-deck: 'many rooms which on other ships would have no outside ventilation, on the *Aquitania* are called "inside-outside" rooms for the fact that a high window opens out of doors on the deck above.' (Author's collection)

An impressive second-class smoke room. (Author's collection)

One of the third-class dining saloons. Unlike first- and second class, the swivel seats were bolted firmly to the deck. (*The Shipbuilder*, 1914/author's collection)

The enclosed third-class promenade area, aft on D-deck. Sheltered from the rain, the open sides permitted a sea view. (By courtesy of the University of Liverpool Library, Cunard Archive)

since the removal of the necessary carpeting and furniture to reveal the dance floor was tiring work in the summer. On both legs of the maiden voyage, the garden lounges were popular, but since the smoking side was always occupied by 100 passengers 'almost all the day' and the non-smoking side 'had very few passengers', it appeared sensible to allow smoking in both lounges on each side of the ship. The long gallery had been 'greatly appreciated by the passengers' and had been used as a lounge and an area for card games. Additional ventilation was required in the barber's shop and typist's office adjoining the long gallery. Passengers appeared satisfied with the first-class smoke room, although the centre portion of the floor underneath the carpet needed to be planed. The lighting was 'exceedingly good', so much so that the chandelier was not needed. Before lunch or dinner, passengers congregated in the foyer, but in general the foyer was 'not used to any large extent'. In the first-class dining saloon, the number of chairs proved insufficient when there was a large complement of passengers. Seventy-five chairs needed to be ordered for the room, while some of the joints in the lino needed relaying. The passengers were pleased with the grill room, although on the eastbound leg of the maiden voyage it had been was necessary to take some of the tables from the second-class dining saloon. Twenty more chairs needed to be ordered. An average of seventy-five passengers used the ship's swimming bath each day, while the bath and gymnasium were 'greatly appreciated by the passengers'. First-class staterooms needed attention as there were a number of hooks, shelves, water bottle holders and mirrors which needed adding. Several passengers complained that 'the beds were not as comfortable as they might be', and it was thought that it might be necessary to alter the tension of the springs. Passenger accommodation ventilation 'worked exceedingly well' overall, with the exception of one section, although on the westbound leg of the maiden voyage there were several floods 'owing to the ventilators being turned head to the storm'. The relatively small defects were a testament to the quality of the ship's design.

Aquitania's second Liverpool departure came as soon as 20 June 1914, and she was to arrive back in her home port on 7 July 1914 after a successful round trip to New York. For the voyage to New York, there were 1,408 passengers (351 first class, 439 second class and 618 third class). Leonard Peskett was on board to record the new ship in action. On the westbound leg, the weather was fine overall, although there was a heavy swell early in the voyage which caused the ship to pitch a little and roll – under three degrees – but 'neither movement was sufficient to cause any inconvenience or unpleasantness'. Although the Frahm's anti-rolling tanks were operating for the entire voyage, 'the weather conditions were not such as to give the vessel any severe test.' In general it was thought that Aquitania 'would prove to be an excellent sea boat in any weather'. By the time she arrived in New York, she had averaged 23.2 knots. There were some passenger complaints about ventilation, but nothing that could not be remedied by the installation of additional fans. There were some problems noted with the crew's galley, which required enlargement, while the first-class gallery layout and equipment needed improvement since it had been 'taxed to its utmost capacity'. Upon arrival in New York, some changes were made. Several first-class rooms were fitted with new wardrobes, while Peskett drew up a list of additional rooms where wardrobes needed to be fitted. For the eastbound leg, 2,515 passengers were aboard (752 first class, 614 second class and 1,149 third class) alongside 1,083 crew, to make a grand total of 3,598 people. With the current in her favour, Aquitania's speed improved compared to the westbound crossing.

By the end of her third round trip, 11,208 passengers had been carried at an average of 1,868 passengers on each crossing. Aquitania was proving popular, yet her civilian career was rudely interrupted by the outbreak of the First World War. It would be another six years before she returned to passenger service.

NOTES

1 *Shipbuilder* 2, page 211.
2 *Shipbuilder* 2, op. cit.
3 *Shipbuilder* 2, op. cit.

three

IN HIS MAJESTY'S SERVICE

By 5 August 1914 the Admiralty had called up *Aquitania* and *Caronia* for war service, stating their intention to requisition *Lusitania*, *Mauretania* and *Carmania* when they returned to port. Fourteen days later Cunard were informed that *Lusitania* and *Mauretania* would not be required, but before then *Aquitania* had left the River Mersey 'for patrol duty' as an armed merchant cruiser on 8 August 1914.[1] Many of *Aquitania*'s luxury fittings had been removed: 'Guns were mounted on her decks fore and aft, and a naval captain was put in command with a crew of bluejackets and marines', according to one newspaper report. The ship's company numbered 661, with four 6-in guns on the forecastle, four on B-deck and four on C-deck. They had actually been on board before the war's outbreak.

Aquitania's service was marred by a collision with the liner *Canadian* on the morning of 22 August 1914. The log reported 'passing through patches of fog at intervals' before the accident:

7.06. Lat. 50°20′ N Long. 17°30′ W sighted SS Canadian bearing 310°. Steering 90°.

7.07. A/C [altered course] to 340[°] to close.

7.09. Helm hard a port and slow.

7.10. Stopped.

7.11. Full speed astern.

7.13. Collided starb. Side abaft engine room, engines slow ahead W.T. [watertight] doors closed. Sea boats called away. Lifeboats cleared away to lower.

7.22 Engines astern to examine damage.

7.30. Carpenter employed strengthening bulkheads. Hands cleaning, forepeak damage: – stem buckled and plates torn away from 5 feet down and aft to [hull] frame 304.

Word of the collision reached New York on 24 August 1914, with a Lloyd's dispatch from Liverpool reporting that *Aquitania* – 'painted black, including the funnels' – had anchored in the Mersey with a damaged bow. It was hard to keep secrets. Yet it did not take long for it to become apparent that liners of the *Aquitania*'s size were simply unsuitable as armed merchant cruisers. Not only did they have a large appetite for coal, which was required for the war effort, but their size and relatively limited manoeuvrability were hardly ideal. Early in September 1914, the Admiralty informed Cunard that her service would end on 30 September 1914, and there was necessary 'repair and restoration work' which had to be completed before she was discharged from service.

After months of idleness, *Aquitania* was called upon again. This time it was for troopship service. She was involved in a mishap when she grounded in the river Mersey on 26 May 1915. This was probably the incident John Clifford described to his brother, Leslie Morton (a survivor of *Lusitania*'s sinking). Clifford was at the helm while *Aquitania* was moving from the 'Gladstone drydock to go alongside the Prince's landing stage'. Obeying an order to turn to starboard, *Aquitania* mysteriously 'took a wide sheer to port' and the bow from ahead of the bridge ended up hard aground. Morton recalled: 'I later heard that the cause of the accident was suspected sabotage, as an "outside" in double-ended spanners was later found in the telemotor gear aft which has [sic] caused it not only to jam, but to reverse when [the] port helm [i.e. a turn to starboard] was put on her.'[2] If it was sabotage, it did not take her out of service for too long, yet bow damage traceable to a grounding in the Mersey would be apparent for years afterwards, and Morton's description of the circumstances rings true.

Aquitania made several voyages to the Dardanelles between May and August 1915, conveying around 30,000 troops.[3] Regimental Quarter Master Sergeant

Aquitania's crowded decks during the war. The raised portion of the promenade deck, allowing a better view of the sea, was removed when the first-class accommodation was extended after 1926. (J. & C. McCutcheon collection)

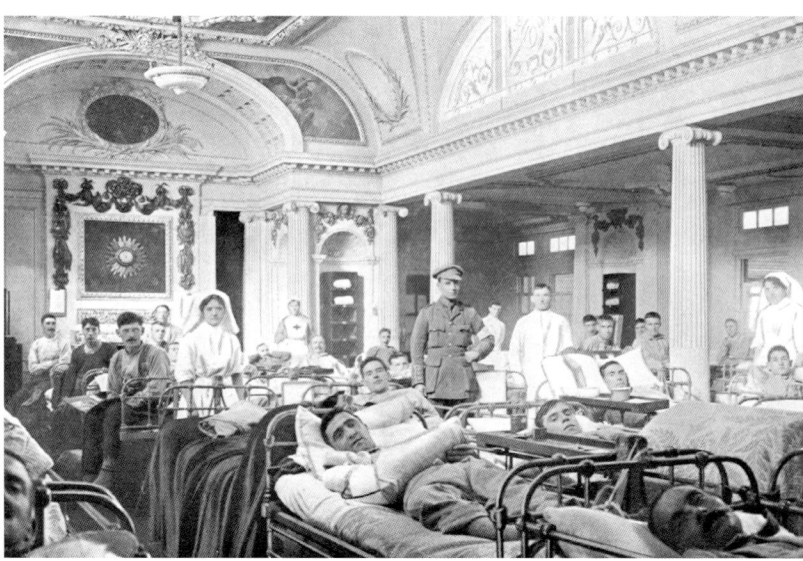

The first-class lounge as it appeared during the liner's hospital service. (J. & C. McCutcheon collection)

Edward Miles boarded the *Aquitania* at Liverpool on the late afternoon of 28 June 1915, and found the ship's accommodation 'most ample'.[4] His initial excitement on finding that the *Aquitania* was underway turned to a slight disappointment when he discovered that they were only leaving the dock, and would remain in the river Mersey until noon on 3 July 1915. Accompanied by three torpedo boat destroyers, *Aquitania* proceeded down the Mersey and into the St George's Channel. She 'quickly gathered speed'. Miles thought *Aquitania* had reached 26 knots by the time Ireland came into view, which would have been very creditable. He had mixed feelings as his home country vanished from sight, writing that although he was 'far from a sentimentalist', 'the dear ones you are leaving behind, not knowing how long it may be before you will again clasp the hands of those to whom you are devoted, and, on the other hand, the duty which lies before you, one which every Briton's son should be proud to perform.'

While sailing a zigzag course to avoid submarines, *Aquitania* was developing a steady roll, and the danger was highlighted the next morning when Miles was awoken early (around 6 a.m.) by several men running past his cabin putting on lifebelts. 'It transpired that a torpedo had been discharged at us from a hostile submarine, but, fortunately for us, missed its target by a matter of a few feet', he wrote.

Kapitänleutnant Walter Forstmann's *U-39* was the only U-boat in the vicinity – estimated position 49°45′ North 8°50′ West. Unaware of *Aquitania*'s identity, her log recorded: 'dived in front of a large steamer, which was on a zigzag course.' Yet Forstmann underestimated the distance and the failed attack cost him his final torpedo.[5]

Breakfast was adequate: porridge, eggs and bacon, and a whole pint of coffee. After spending time reading on deck and relaxing in a deckchair as he watched the sun set, Miles pondered, 'It is hard to believe that we are engaged in, what may be, the longest and most terrible war the world has ever known.' At a time when the First World War was less than a year old, Miles' words showed considerable foresight. On 6 July 1915, Gibraltar came into view at around 11 a.m., although a slight haze worked against seeing anything more than the outline. In the hotter climate, that evening the troops were allowed to sleep out on deck, since the bunks were 'almost unbearable in the heat', although a shock awaited Miles at 1 a.m. – he was awoken by another soldier who was worried that the ship was sinking. Fortunately, there was a less dramatic explanation for the 3in of water on the boat deck: the deck scrubbers were at work! Malta came into view on the morning of Thursday, 8 July 1915, and by the Saturday morning *Aquitania* was entering Mudros, on the island of Lemnos. Miles saw 'dozens of battle ships, and submarines,

A classic view of *Aquitania* as a hospital ship. The green line highlights the sheer of the decks. (J. & C. McCutcheon collection)

and torpedo boats of all the allied countries in the bay, besides thousands of smaller craft.' At the frighteningly early hour of 4 a.m. on Sunday, the troops all paraded on deck and disembarked, the trip ashore taking ten minutes in the lifeboats. Miles' first impression was 'utter barrenness everywhere. One wonders how anything could grow…' He was a world away from Liverpool, or his home in Witley, Surrey – three miles from Godalming – where he had been just two weeks beforehand.

Private Ernest Lye had enlisted on 28 August 1914 in the Duke of Wellington's West Riding Regiment, undergoing ten months' worth of training before joining the *Aquitania* at Liverpool for her 3 July 1915 departure to Mudros.[6] He described it as a 'great adventure' and remembered: 'We really had no idea where we were bound, but as usual there were plenty of rumours flying around, but seeing that these mentioned nearly every spot under the sun, they could not be relied upon.' He was certainly impressed with the ship, describing her as 'wonderful' and writing that she was:

Aquitania at Mudros. She dwarfs the smaller hospital ships. (Clyde George collection)

Aquitania shown docked at Halifax, in a lovely view of her in 'dazzle' paint. Although a black and white photograph, the viewpoint is reminiscent of Arthur Lismer's wonderful colour painting of *Olympic* (see *RMS* Olympic, Titanic's *sister*). (MacAskill photo from the collection of the Maritime Museum of the Atlantic)

The single-funnelled hospital ship *Voloavia* appears tiny next to her colleague, *Aquitania*. (Author's collection/Michail Michailakis)

Aquitania at New York around 1918. (Author's collection)

… like a marvellous fairy palace that we read about as children. Our battalion found ourselves allocated to second class berths and how we appreciated them after the camp life we had lived. No one could have wished for better food, which we partook of in the second class dining saloon, a beautiful room with a wide staircase leading down to it, and with marble pillars supporting the roof. There were bathrooms situated but a few doors away from the cabin, which I shared with one of our men, and we made good use of the hot or cold sea or fresh water that could be drawn from the taps, particularly when we reached the Mediterranean and found a sun hotter than we had ever known it before.

He remembered that the voyage was 'a happy one, with sports and parades being the order of the day, although parades were very few and far between'. Due to the heat, and the regulation that portholes were to be closed at night ('no lights had to be shown'), the cabins were unbearably hot 'and for the rest of the voyage we slept on deck'. All in all, there were nine battalions of infantry onboard, along with units such as those from the Royal Army Medical Corps.

Lye calculated that there were almost 5,700 troops on board, and, writing in the 1920s, reflected, 'I suppose some of us were too young to think of anything but the glorious present and little thought of the great gamble we were to take

Another image of *Aquitania* in dazzle, this view looking forward on the port side. (From the collection of the Maritime Museum of the Atlantic)

part in, and that many of those who were lining the rails of that great steamer were never to see their "homeland" again.' After arriving in Mudros harbour on the island of Lemnos, it was only after a day had passed that *Aquitania*'s complement disembarked. 'It was the first time that many of us, including myself, had ever set foot on soil other than dear "Old England", which now seemed so far away.'

Private G.A. Handford was in the same regiment as Lye, and remembered that same voyage.[7] He wrote in his diary that the 'wonderful Cunard liner *Aquitania* looked like some huge city and as majestic as she did gigantic. On her, we soon found out our surprises, for she has many spacious decks, and also a magnificent supply of lifeboats.' Handford remembered an incident 'at about 5 a.m.' on the second day at sea:

As soon as our escort had left us some energetic lookout reported the fact that a submarine was visible and almost immediately the said submarine – which was afterwards known to be of the Austrian type – fired a torpedo at us but luckily missed us by three yards astern. But what a sensation it caused, for almost as soon as this transpired the buglers sounded the 'alarm' and inside of a minute everybody were [sic] on deck with their life belts on and securely fitted and standing ready for the next words of command. Rolls were called, an inspection was held and finally after about eight hours of this vigil we were dismissed …

Aquitania took a zigzag course, leaving the submarine far behind, Handford remembered – 'for they could not keep up to the 28½ knots an hour that our ship was capable of and was at the time doing.' Handford's estimate would have fitted the *Mauretania*'s performance rather than the *Aquitania*'s, yet it was only two months since the *Lusitania* had been torpedoed and sunk and it was fortunate that *Aquitania* came through unscathed.

Edgar Britten, who joined the *Aquitania* as her staff captain early in 1915, remembered the same voyage.[8] He recalled the 'alarm bell on the bridge tinkled sharply', as the after lookout warned, 'Torpedo, sir. Passed within fifty feet of our stern.' It was still a close shave, if not the three yards that Handford had been told. 'What a prize to miss by a bare fifty feet, the finest ship afloat, with an army aboard', Britten wrote years later:

Even now I can picture that U-boat commander, his eyes glued to the periscope, gazing in consternation as he saw the wake of his torpedo swirling harmlessly past our stern. But he would be after us. Come, old lady, that extra burst of speed for which you are famous, for on that alone depends the lives of 6,000 men. The *Aquitania* did not fail.

Above: Arthur Lismer's 1919 painting entitled 'The Transport *Aquitania*'. (Canadian War Museum, Beaverbrook Collection of War Art)

Above left and left: Two rare photos of USS *Shaw* after the collision. The photographer mistook *Olympic* for *Aquitania*! (Darren Clossin collection)

While their largest ship came through her adventures safely, Cunard had to pay attention to more mundane matters. *Aquitania*'s payment as a military transport, from 11 May 1915, stood at fifteen shillings per gross ton every month. From 26 June 1915 a flat payment of £10,000 each month for the ship was fixed, yet by 23 August 1915 the rate changed again to ten shillings per gross ton each month. For the *Aquitania* this came to around £22,820. Just over a year into the war, however, times were changing and she would soon find herself serving in another capacity.

As demand for hospital ships increased due to the Dardanelles campaign, the decision was taken late in August 1915 to begin fitting-out the *Aquitania* as a hospital ship from 4 September 1915. All in all, the cost of conversion to a troopship and then a hospital ship came to around £63,000. By the time the Dardanelles were evacuated, the need for hospital ships diminished, and in February 1916 it was arranged with Cunard that *Aquitania*'s fittings would be kept intact so that she could be ready for service at a later date, at half the rate of hire. Strangely enough, the War Office asked the Ministry of Transport to discharge *Aquitania* entirely and on 10 April 1916 she was withdrawn for reconditioning at Southampton, Cunard being offered £90,000. In fact, £57,000 represented the cost of the reconditioning work itself, while the remaining £33,000 represented three months' hire.

Yet in a matter of months it became clear to the Ministry of Transport that *Aquitania* was needed again; on 21 July 1916 orders were issued to reconvert *Aquitania* to a hospital ship. Even in wartime bureaucracy was evident, as there was a question mark hanging over what proportion of the reconditioning costs awarded to Cunard could be reclaimed by the government. The question arose because the ship's reconditioning had not been completed by the time she was required again as a hospital ship. On 21 November 1916, the same day that the White Star Line's *Britannic* had been sunk by a suspected mine in the Aegean Sea while serving as a hospital ship, *Aquitania* was ordered to proceed to the Mediterranean, leaving Southampton in early December 1916. By the end of the month she was laid up in the Solent, still outfitted as a hospital ship, where she stayed for the whole of 1917, in spite of losing 'an anchor and 120 fathoms of cable' during high winds in November that year.[9] Following the German announcement of unrestricted submarine warfare, a memo from the War Office in April 1917 had stated that *Aquitania*'s size rendered her 'a magnificent target for torpedoes' and noted she was 'unable to use most of the harbours in the Mediterranean. Since the German notice, she cannot use unprotected anchorages, and if she should still be employed on hospital service, her loss would simply be a matter of time … she must be withdrawn from hospital service.' The British Government's understandable concern signalled the end

of that phase of employment and probably saved *Aquitania* from a premature end.

All in all, *Aquitania* had 'carried a total of no fewer than 25,000 wounded troops' during her time as a hospital ship.[10] Lieutenant Harold Blake fondly remembered his first glimpse of the *Aquitania* at Lemnos, having convinced one of the field hospital doctors that he was healthy enough to make the journey back home:[11] 'I was placed on a stretcher and laid on the ground to await my turn to be taken aboard the hospital ship.' He wrote:

I knew this to be the *Aquitania*, and looked eagerly across the harbour at her. I had once seen her leaving the Mersey just before the war and had then been greatly attracted by her graceful yet powerful appearance. I little realised how very soon my wish would be granted or under what changed conditions I should see her again. She didn't now bear much resemblance to the ship I had seen only a year before, for instead of the well-known Cunard colours, she was painted white and had a huge red cross on her hull, but she was even more attractive than before and I longed to get on board.

There was some disappointment, since the sea was 'very rough' and the men had to wait on the shore for an entire day without food or drink, before being told to make their way back to the hospitals just before it went dark. Blake struggled on his hands and knees before he collapsed and an RAMC sergeant helped him into an ambulance. It was two days before he boarded the *Aquitania*, 'convinced that my recovery started from that time and by the time we reached Naples I was taking an interest in food and anticipating my arrival in England. I was still too weak to be allowed up, but the doctor allowed me to have [a] light diet and also ordered a bottle of stout each day.' Unfortunately, Blake's appetite got the better of him and he disobeyed orders by sneaking into the dining room and indulging, yet that evening the doctor realised what he had done and put him on a 'milk diet' before he even had a chance to drink any stout. He described his voyage as 'quite uneventful' prior to arriving at Southampton, where he was carried to a train to be taken to a large hospital on the outskirts of London. 'It was very difficult to realise that I was within a few hours' journey of home. Gallipoli had seemed to be on the other side of the world, and when there, England seemed to be an inaccessible place that I would probably never see again', he wrote in his diary.

Even though she was now laid up in the Solent, *Aquitania*'s name was dragged into disrepute as a result of allegations surrounding the use of the ship in 1915, which the German government published in a 1917 list of alleged misuse of British hospital ships. An anonymous Dutchman alleged, 'The *Aquitania*, which left the port of Naples at 8.30 on 29 November, and passed by the Kavi at a distance of forty meters was chock-full of British soldiers, none of whom were wounded.' It was a serious charge to make, since the use of a hospital ship to transport healthy troops would be a breach of the Geneva convention. The soldiers were merely 'non-cot cases' according to the British Government – troops who were not confined to bed and wore khaki, since according to the regulations there was no requirement for 'non-cot cases' to wear the blue hospital suits. Yet another allegation surfaced from a Norwegian ship's captain who said that he had seen 'the British hospital ship *Aquitania* leave [Liverpool] in a fog on 7 December 1915, with 1,500 men and all accessories onboard; she was, in particular, carrying cavalry.' Britain replied that since the *Aquitania* had been at Naples on 29 November 1915, even at top speed it would have been impossible to have reached Liverpool, disembarked passengers, taken on coal, taken on stores, prepared to depart, embarked more passengers, and then sailed again in the time available. In fact, replying to the allegations, the Admiralty declared, '*Aquitania* was *not* [original emphasis] at Liverpool at all in December 1915. She arrived at Southampton on 3 December, disembarked her patients, and was prepared for further service as quickly as possible, leaving Southampton on 16 December for Mudros.'[12]

If the accusations against *Aquitania* could be consigned to history, her war service was still very much in the present. Once America entered the war on the Allied side, even more hard work beckoned for her. Britten remembered *Aquitania* returning to service early in 1918, for she was to make nine trips across the Atlantic and carry no fewer than 60,000 American troops to Europe.[13]

Captain James T.W. Charles was in command when one of the most unfortunate accidents of *Aquitania*'s career occurred. On the morning of 9 October 1918, *Aquitania* was sailing in convoy to Southampton at around 22 knots. Charles later said that there were around 5,500 troops onboard – 'considerably less than usual, on account of sickness' – and 'a crew of about 900'. Captain William A. Glassford, of the United States Navy's USS *Shaw*, was the Escort Commander of the division of five American destroyers accompanying the convoy to Southampton. At daybreak that morning, around fifty miles to the south-west of Portland Bill, Glassford was awoken and gave orders for the escorts to assume their proper positions: *Kimberley* on the *Aquitania*'s starboard bow; *Duncan* two miles ahead of the convoy, and the *Conyngham* between three and four miles ahead.

Glassford was concerned that 'conditions were extremely favourable in very dangerous waters for a submarine attack on my convoy.' He said that 'the light was good but there still lingered the grey of the early dawn, and I considered that such a moment was a very propitious one for such an attack.' Glassford had ordered full speed ahead so that the *Shaw* could take up her position around 1,000 yards off the *Aquitania*'s port bow. Unaware of when *Aquitania* was due to begin her zigzag course, he 'went ahead of her about 1,500 yards and checked her course as approximately ninety degrees off her base course.' Glassford 'sheered to the left' to begin zigzagging, which he judged to be necessary until the conditions had become less favourable to a submarine attack. After completing the first left leg, events took an unfortunate turn:

I … gave the order 'right rudder' and swung in a wide circle to the right, and was on a course approximately thirty-five degrees converging to the course of the *Aquitania* and 1,000 yards or more broad on her port bow, when I ordered the rudder to be put to left to commence my left leg of the zigzag. The helmsman immediately reported that the rudder had jammed. I looked at the rudder indicator and saw that it was jammed at seventeen or eighteen degrees right rudder. As soon as the rudder jammed it was very apparent to me that the *Aquitania* was in a very precarious situation and my immediate concern was for her safety and for the safety of the troops onboard of her. Should I hold my speed and make a run for it there was a danger either of ramming the *Aquitania* at full speed and sinking her, or having her crash into my stern, where were my depth charges [sic]. This would have caused a terrible disaster. I judged that by backing there was less danger to her and incidentally, to myself. These contingencies flashed through my mind, and having made the decision, I reversed my engines emergency astern, and stood to wait for the consequences, which were not long in coming, the *Aquitania* crashing into my bow, as I expected.

Captain Charles, who had been in the small chart room on the bridge for the entire night, was on *Aquitania*'s bridge prior to the collision:

I saw the *Shaw* on my port bow at a distance of about 500 yards, crossing at a dangerous angle. She was blowing her whistle continuously. Previous to my coming out of the chart room, the *Aquitania*'s helm had been put hard-a-port. I saw that a collision was inevitable, and gave orders: 'all bulkhead doors to be closed', and immediately after, the collision occurred.

Aquitania hit the *Shaw* immediately in front of her bridge on the starboard side, at an angle of about forty degrees. Yet the speeding liner's momentum enabled her to slice through the *Shaw*'s hull, cutting her in two. *Shaw* scraped along the liner's port side and tore away the lifeboat hanging from the twenty-fourth set of davits. Amazingly, only two rivets had been loosened near *Aquitania*'s stem. Yet for the *Shaw*, the consequences were catastrophic – as Glassford recounted:

…a large gash was cut in my side approximately twenty feet by four feet, a little distance above the waterline, in my forward boiler room, on the port side. My mainmast went by the board and fell over the starboard counter. The fore part of the ship was immediately in flames, due in my opinion to the flash of sparks at impact igniting the oil in my forward tanks. I ordered the life rafts to be put in the water, and directed that the forward magazine be flooded before I left the bridge, which was in flames. I do not exactly remember how I got off the bridge. I directed the quartermaster to in some way signal to the *Duncan* which had stood over near me, to rescue people from my then floating bow, about 200 yards away. This word also got to the *Kimberley*, and not a few officers and men were recovered from this bow. My immediate concern at this time was the probability of an explosion in my forward magazine, and an intense oil fire was raging forward surrounding the magazine…

Shaw's drifting bow floated on an even keel for some time, settling down at the after end as it flooded, so that some of the men trapped on it thought that the whole ship was intact. They swam away in the knowledge that there were depth charges in the stern. Two commissioned officers and ten enlisted men lost their lives. 'Their loss was in the line of duty', Glassford testified. 'I cannot say exactly how they met their end.'

By 16 October 1918, a naval investigation in Portsmouth concluded that nobody was to blame. *Shaw*'s helm had jammed, thereby causing the collision, yet that was a mechanical fault rather than any human error. 'All necessary precautions' had been taken to maintain the steering gear and auxiliary machinery, which had been checked half an hour prior to the collision. Glassford had taken 'all necessary precautions' after the collision to flood the magazines, 'render the depth charges safe', put the fire out and shore up watertight bulkheads onboard the *Shaw*.

With the war over, by 15 December 1918 *Aquitania* arrived at Liverpool to enter the Gladstone dock; by 10 January 1919 she had left government service.[14] While no longer under the white ensign, *Aquitania* remained under government charter and made a number of voyages before her arrival back at Southampton on 2 August 1919. Some first-class areas were restored, yet second and third remained spartan. *Aquitania* made a round trip to New York, leaving on 18 September 1919 for Liverpool. Before she settled back into peacetime service, a thorough overhaul at Tyneside beckoned, especially since Cunard had decided to convert her boilers to burn oil.

The conversion required 95½ tons of rivets, and 11,300 yards of steel piping. 800 men were initially employed, the total increasing to 2,500 men over time. Perhaps the main improvement was that oil could be supplied continuously to the burners in the boiler furnaces. All in all, there were 168 furnaces, and as a coal burner, the equivalent of 8,000 horsepower could have been lost every four hours, assuming twenty-eight furnaces required cleaning on each watch. As an oil burner, theoretically the ship's speed would improve, while coal dust would be eliminated.[15]

By the time the refit was completed she was 'as spick and span as the day she first sailed from the Mersey.' The *Cunard Magazine* recorded, 'The Tyne gave a rousing send-off and its fleet of trawlers made day fearsome and the coming night to be dreaded by its jubilant improvisation of discords upon a hundred sirens of different tones.'

NOTES

1 Britten, page 72.

2 Morton, pages 118–19.

3 Britten, op. cit.

4 Details of Regimental Quarter Master Edward Miles' voyage taken from Imperial War Museum (henceforth referred to as IWM) reference 83/6/1.

5 My sincere thanks for information to Michael Lowrey and Oliver Lörscher. See Bundesarchiv-Militärarchiv, reference RM 97/802. I also appreciate Günter Bäbler's translation.

6 Details of Private Ernest Lye's voyage taken from IWM reference 81/91/1.

7 Details of Private G.A. Handford's voyage taken from IWM reference 90/21/1.

8 Britten, pages 73–74.

9 McCart's *Atlantic Liners*, page 103.

10 Britten, page 73.

11 Details of Lieutenant Harold Blake's voyage taken from IWM reference 03/15/1.

12 *Correspondence With The German Government Regarding The Alleged Misuse Of British Hospital Ships*, London: His Majesty's Stationary Office; 1917.

13 Britten, page 73.

14 McCart's *Atlantic Liners*, op. cit.

15 *Aquitania*'s anti-rolling tanks became oil bunkers after the war, as Cunard confirmed late in October 1920 that the conversion work begun at Newcastle had been completed at New York.

four

THE 'SHIP BEAUTIFUL'

By 28 June 1920, *Aquitania* was back in her home port, getting ready to sail for New York on 17 July 1920. During the trip from Newcastle, round the north of Scotland, she had attained a speed of more than 24.5 knots. There was even speculation that she might try and capture the Blue Riband, highlighting the rush of optimism as Cunard's 'Ship Beautiful' returned to service. Her popularity was set to rise to new heights. Charles Spedding, appointed as *Aquitania*'s purser when she returned to service after the war, remembered:

> The *Aquitania* was not going to be an Atlantic ferry; she was going to be a palace of enjoyment. People would not look upon her simply as a means of transport to the places where they intended to enjoy a holiday; the *Aquitania* was to be a part of their holiday, and a prominent part of their enjoyment.[1]

There was considerable interest about the refit in America, and the *New York Times* noted some of the improvements:

> On D-deck, in the reception room opposite the great restaurant, a bank and inquiry office or information bureau have been installed. To the swimming bath and gymnasium have been added a big sunbath room. The staterooms on the boat deck have been converted into one-berth rooms, each fitted with a bed and settee, and the whole of C-deck amidships has been completely rebuilt. The staterooms have been greatly enlarged and in order to obtain this result the original accommodation has been reduced to thirty-two rooms. Many of these staterooms now have private dressing rooms.

Gleaming and polished, the ship's interiors appeared as new as they had in 1914. The *Cunard Magazine* published 'a lady visitor's' account of the liner,

identifying her only by the initials 'I.V.W.'. Touring the liner at Liverpool, she first saw the first-class dining saloon – complete with the dust sheets that had not been removed:

> Everything struck me as being in such good taste … Nothing gaudy, saving the newly-gilt design on the black railings of the stairway and the lift gates … I liked the subdued tones in the tapestry, the beautiful blends of dull blues and other artistic shades. The whole atmosphere was one of refinement, with nothing of the *noveau riche* about it. The chairs and settees were obviously made for comfort, and were so cosily set together. Nothing was stilted or formal in the arrangement of the furniture.

She was 'enraptured with the suites that have their own little veranda on the deck – I thought it was a priceless arrangement'.

If there had been any doubts as to the ship's popularity after the war, these were dispelled by a glance at the passenger list, which included no fewer than 2,433 passengers. Her best day's run during the voyage stood at 576 miles, an average speed of around 24 knots. Cunard's Supervising Engineer John Austin noted that *Aquitania* had burned 610 tons of oil daily, whereas she had previously burned 960 tons of coal (presumably at full speed). On her arrival in New York, *Aquitania*'s accommodation impressed a reporter, who liked the first-class dining saloon: 'The colour scheme has been changed and the red and gold decorations in the dining room have disappeared. The present scheme is of the Pompeian period and restful to the eye.' Yet the voyage had been marred by a terrible accident on 19 July 1920, when there was an explosion of one of the main steam pipes. Fireman James Curran suffered burns and Assistant Engineer Scott Barkway died as a result of his injuries.

Atlantic Liner in Gladstone Dock, Seaforth.

Above: Postmarked 12 October 1920. Although the caption reads 'Atlantic liner in Gladstone Dock', *Aquitania*'s name and Liverpool – her port of registry – are clearly visible at the stern. (Author's collection)

Above right: *Aquitania*'s fresh, gleaming white paint gives her an impressive profile. Taken in June 1920, this photograph shows her at Liverpool; between the liner's first and second funnels, one of the Liver birds can be seen in the background on top of the clock tower. (Clyde George collection)

Centre right: Thick smoke belching from her funnels, *Aquitania*'s formidable bulk is evident. (J. & C. McCutcheon collection)

Below right: Docked at Southampton in the 1920s, *Aquitania*'s rival – the White Star Line's *Majestic* – can be seen on the extreme right. (J. & C. McCutcheon collection)

Above: The graceful lines of *Aquitania*'s hull were admirable from many angles. Here she is shown at Southampton on a bright sunny day. The open sides of the third-class promenade area, on D-deck near the stern, are visible (see an interior photograph on page 25); note the white-painted webframes with the round openings. They were located on every third frame and added considerably to the hull's strength. (J. Kent Layton collection)

Above left: An undoubtedly unique, yet scratched, photo of *Aquitania* docked at Southampton in the late 1920s. (J. & C. McCutcheon collection)

Centre left: *Aquitania*'s starboard bow, part of a unique snap from a private album. (J. & C. McCutcheon collection)

Below left: On the left, White Star's *Majestic*, and on the right, *Berengaria* – *Aquitania*'s running mate. Both were ex-German liners, for *Majestic* had been launched in 1914 as HAPAG's *Bismarck*. (Author's collection)

Below: *Aquitania* at Southampton. The liner to her right seems to be *Majestic*. (Author's collection)

Staff Captain F. E. Storey read the service at his funeral, before he was buried at sea. Such unfortunate accidents were all too common at the time.

When *Aquitania* departed from New York on 31 July 1920, the eastbound crossing would take her back to Southampton, as Cunard had switched their main express service from Liverpool. She had a healthy passenger list, and her 686 first-class, 637 second-class and 862 third-class passengers brought in revenues of £59,555, £22,524 and £21,139 respectively. Third-class passengers did help fill the ship, but they did not make her pay her way. All in all, by the end of the round voyage she had earned £183,460 – adding up to a net profit of £17,912. By the time she reached Cherbourg, she had covered 3,285 miles in six days, one hour and twelve minutes – an average speed of 22.6 knots. One newspaper report claimed that the final 129 miles had been covered in only three hours and forty-two minutes – an average speed of 27.4 knots, surpassing 'all records for speed of merchant ships.' Tellingly, the time and distance figures did not add up. Yet regardless of the truth of that story, *Aquitania*'s performance was pleasing, with her best day's run of 548 miles giving an average of fractionally under 24 knots. (Due to time changes, an eastbound day was shorter than a westbound one.) There did not seem to be any stopping the rumours circulating in papers such as the *New York Times*, where Captain Charles and William Albert White, the inventor of the low-pressure oil-feed machinery, were quoted as being confident that '*Aquitania* would beat all the Atlantic records for speed with her new fuel'.

By the time *Aquitania* arrived in New York after her second westbound crossing as an oil-burning liner, she had a passenger list of 2,637 as her

This nice atmospheric image shows *Aquitania* at Southampton's Berth 50. During the June 1924 opening of Southampton's new floating dry dock (also sometimes called a 'floating dock'), built by Armstrong Whitworth, the Union Castle liner *Windsor Castle* was apparently the first liner in. Proud reports described the new dry dock as the 'greatest in the world', pointing out that it was designed and built in Britain. (Eric Longo Image Collection)

Cutaways showing liners' interiors were a popular form of promotion. Showing the extent of the accommodation, as well as the vast interiors, *Aquitania* appears no less than a floating town. (Clyde George collection)

Assisted by tugs, *Aquitania* comes into port at Southampton. The curve of her bow is reminiscent of *Lusitania*, yet *Aquitania*'s superstructure appears 'boxy' from this viewpoint, almost as if it is too large for the hull beneath it. (J. & C. McCutcheon collection)

This rare view includes Cunard's three express liners, all in port at the same time in the early 1930s. While *Aquitania*, *Berengaria* and *Mauretania* are shown, only White Star's *Majestic* and *Homeric* are visible. The other member of the White Star Line's express trio, *Olympic*, was not in port. Although the three White Star liners had a higher gross tonnage than each of their Cunard counterparts, Cunard's liners had a higher combined average speed. (Author's collection)

Right: Tourist-third-class passengers relax on the deck in July 1929. (J. & C. McCutcheon collection)

Below right: An interesting photograph of *Aquitania*'s starboard bridge from 1928. The unidentified officer is taking a bearing with a pelorus. As with all of the ship's docking, steering and anchor telegraphs, the telegraph in the background was supplied and fitted by Messrs. A. Robinson & Co. of Bootle, Liverpool. The telegraph's dials were 24in in diameter, while the port and starboard telegraph handles could be operated independently whenever it was necessary. All in all, 12,000ft 'of specially annealed steel wire' was used to connect all of the ship's telegraph instruments together. (J. & C. McCutcheon collection)

Below: Smoking a pipe on deck, 1919. (J. & C. McCutcheon collection)

Left: Tennis on deck, 1929. The original captioned 'Cpt. Diggle and Fl Wills.' (J. & C. McCutcheon collection)

Above: This photograph of a boxing match taking place on *Aquitania*'s after decks shows the extremity of the stern, while the decks are crowded with spectators watching the match in apparently calm seas and sunny weather. It appears to date from the mid-1930s, perhaps 1933 or 1934. (Author's collection/Eric Longo-Joseph Spletzer Image Collection)

popularity kept rising. When she arrived in New York on 30 October 1920 after a stormy crossing, her passenger list reportedly consisted of no fewer than 2,865 passengers (674 first class, 732 second class and 1,459 third class). In a heavy gale one evening, one huge wave 'rolled over the port bow and smashed five of the big ports in the dining saloon, crushing the glass into fine pieces.' Amazingly, nobody was injured, but little could deter passengers. Her popularity was going to be with her for years to come.

Aquitania was finally enjoying settling into her regular service. However, even during the 'boom years' of the early 1920s, there were times when they hardly seemed like halcyon days. In May 1921, *Aquitania*'s sailing from Southampton

was threatened by a stewards' strike. That was the last thing Cunard needed. While Captain Sir James Charles confidently declared to reporters on 13 May 1921 that 'we are going dead on time at 1 o'clock tomorrow', some thought his confidence was misplaced. Many of Cunard's shore staff volunteered to make the sailing, including none other than Sir Percy Bates. In the event, he 'was not needed', according to the *New York Times*. However, the following day no fewer than 644 stewards sailed, about 180 of them volunteers from Cunard's clerical staff. Despite the union's strike orders, a large number of stewards had signed on anyway. During the voyage, there were a few breeches of protocol for those not used to their temporary jobs. It was reported that 'one Cunard executive, on hearing a lady passenger ask a gentleman companion at the dinner table for a cigarette, quickly replied: "Here, have one of mine."' One passenger, whose wife was apparently seasick, asked for some cereal, haddock and other breakfast foods to be brought to his cabin. Unfortunately, the 'rookie' steward was one of Cunard's executives and he was blunt in telling him, 'Your wife is not seasick. She is spoofing you. Go back and make her get up!' When *Aquitania* docked in New York, around 1,000 sympathisers for the strikers jeered, necessitating a police presence. According to the *New York Times*, there were 2,720 passengers on board, yet reports that *Aquitania* carried a post-war record number of passengers westbound were mistaken. She had carried 3,096 passengers on one crossing in 1920. Whether it was a record or not, *Aquitania* went on to carry an average of just over 2,000 passengers on each crossing in 1921.

By 1923, competition on the Atlantic had reached full strength. From the summer of 1922 White Star's express service from Southampton to New York was operated with the 56,000-ton *Majestic*, the largest vessel in the world and the most popular liner afloat in 1923; the consistently popular 46,000-ton *Olympic*; and the 34,000-ton *Homeric*, with a reputation for steadiness. *Vaterland*, the second ship of HAPAG's intended pre-war trio, made her maiden voyage as the *Leviathan* in 1923. Cunard's express trio – *Mauretania*, *Aquitania* and *Imperator* (renamed *Berengaria*) – settled into a regular service of sustained popularity.

As more of the large liners entered the express service, the United States' immigration curbs of 1921 and 1924 had an unwelcome influence on passenger numbers. Whereas *Aquitania* had carried a total of 26,331 third-class passengers in both directions in 1921, by the following year this declined to 14,165 passengers, falling to 8,208 in 1925. That year she carried only 2,948 third-class passengers westbound. According to Purser Charles Spedding, *Aquitania*'s crew, which had once numbered nearly 1.200, had been reduced to 1,000 after the conversion to oil fuel, yet with the new immigration quotas 'the steerage business practically ceased and the crew were still further reduced to about 850.'[2] All the liners suffered, yet *Aquitania* continued to be popular with first- and second-class passengers.

Even Lord Pirrie, head of Harland & Wolff (the White Star Line's shipbuilders), commented to Purser Spedding, 'you have made the *Aquitania* the most popular ship in the world; the atmosphere of ocean travel is entirely changed.' Meanwhile, Spedding's book, *Reminiscences of Transatlantic Travellers* (published in 1926), quotes Judge Meyer, who had been involved in running the *Leviathan* for the United States Lines: 'The *Aquitania* is the most popular ship in the world, but it cost me nine million dollars to find it out.'[3] Cunard's pride had a very high reputation and was very popular with the travelling

'Sunset at sea' as *Aquitania* sped westbound, June 1929. (J. & C. McCutcheon collection)

Stormy seas, June 1929. (J. & C. McCutcheon collection)

public, yet in fact the three ex-German sisters often had slightly higher average passenger lists. When she carried a total of more than 60,000 passengers in 1921, *Aquitania*'s record total for the year beat the best post-war years of the *Mauretania*, *Berengaria*, *Olympic*, *Majestic* and *Leviathan* respectively. Even *Leviathan*'s best only stood at just over 40,000 passengers in 1927. Press baron Lord Northcliffe, shown the vast engine room by Chief Engineer George Patterson, had once remarked, 'This is the Rolls-Royce of the seas', but Patterson replied, 'You mean the Rolls-Royce is the *Aquitania* of the road!'[4] Northcliffe wrote an article about his voyage by way of a 'thank you' for being shown around the ship, and in Spedding's words, 'The Cunard Company got a free advertisement that they could not have bought for half a million pounds. He cranked up the merits of the *Aquitania* to the skies, calling her the "Wonder Ship", a name that has stuck to her ever since.'[5] Northcliffe's article, which appeared in the *Daily Mail*, was reprinted by Cunard and issued as an illustrated account:

Nowhere in the world, whether it be in the last word in swift luxurious ships or in the latest American hotels, will you find such comfort, such luxury, such amazing, scrupulous cleanliness in every smallest detail … One hardly knows where to begin a sketch of life onboard the *Aquitania*, so many and so various are the features which call for first claim on one's attention, but I think the almost complete absence of vibration comes first.

In other ships, in which I have sailed for the last forty years, your chief pre-occupation is to dodge vibration. In the *Aquitania* you pass an idle hour of

Above: Aquitania's cinema and theatre, installed during the 1932–33 refit. (J. & C. McCutcheon collection)

Opposite above: Seen here arriving at New York, *Aquitania* comes up the Hudson River in the early 1930s. The caption gives her original gross tonnage. (Clyde George collection)

Opposite below left: The third-class general room was spacious and comfortable by 1914 standards. (*The Shipbuilder*, 1914/author's collection)

Opposite below right: Third-class accommodation looked very different by the early 1930s, as shown in this postcard of the then-third-class lounge. (*The Shipbuilder*, 1914/author's collection)

amusement trying to find … that she is moving at all … It was explained to me with most painstaking kindness by Mr George Patterson, Chief Engineer of the wonder ship, why I search in vain for vibration.

It is quite simple, but I can explain it better if I tell you first about what I can only call the 'most glorious dashboard' of a motorcar in the world. The *Aquitania*'s dashboard, whence everything in this multitudinous box of miraculous machinery is controlled, is all dials and meters and gauges and knobs and handles fit to send every motoring gadget-maniac to the nearest asylum for consuming envyiacs. Among these enchanting dials are four – the great four. As steadily as

Aquitania docked at Southampton in the mid-1930s; behind her lies White Star's *Homeric*, a beloved ship whose short life came to a close in 1936, and on the far right of the photo is the Blue Star Line's *Arandora Star*. Built in 1927, she was less than a third of *Aquitania*'s gross tonnage, and she met a sad end when she was torpedoed and sunk in 1940. (J. & C. McCutcheon collection)

the barometer each records the exact speed in revolutions per minute of the four great screw shafts. When I saw them they stood rock steady, with scarcely a flicker of the needle either way. I made a hasty calculation and said, or rather yelled at the full pitch of my voice, '160?' The chief nodded, signed to an assistant, who did something mysterious, which caused one dial-needle to show 172 and the other 160. I have never felt so conceited in all my life. I had made a fairly accurate shot at the exact propeller speed which was taking us along at between 22 and 23 knots.

Now the secret of the *Aquitania*'s lack of that terrible quiver and vibration we all know so well is simply keeping those four dials as nearly as possible at the same figure. And as you control this mass of force by the mere admission of fuel (not unlike that of a motorcar) by idly fingering a tap or throttle, it is not difficult to make them all read alike and to keep everyone aboard comfortable in their insides.

Northcliffe's child-like joy at seeing the ship's machinery in action gave way to words praising the 'undreamt-of paradise for all suffering housewives', as he called one of the galleys. He praised the third- and second-class menus, which provided ample choice, before mentioning the extensive first-class areas:

The first class passengers of the *Aquitania* have seven or eight places in which to spend the day or parts of it. There is, of course, as might be expected, a simply limitless dining room, where about 700 people are served at the same time, as well as, if not a great deal better than, they would be at home, with food and wine of a kind unobtainable anywhere but in a very, very few West End restaurants and private houses.

The grill room came in for even more praise, and as Northcliffe's article comes to a close it is hard to believe that he wasn't in the pay of Cunard's publicity department!

There are a drawing room of gigantic size, a library, a smoking room full of temptingly enormous sleep-chairs, a Georgian gallery where you can write, another

Above: In April 1935, *Aquitania* ran aground in Southampton water near the Thorn Knoll buoy. Her sleek profile is impressive. (Clyde George collection)

Above left: A lovely, atmospheric image of *Aquitania* at Southampton in the 1930s. (J. & C. McCutcheon collection)

Left: Another Southampton departure. (Clyde George collection)

smaller gallery where you can waste your time in the same way, a magnificent veranda café where nothing but idleness is permitted, with a perfect dancing floor which is busy every night, and, last of all, the Long Gallery. Do you remember the long hall into which Alice in Wonderland fell out of the well in the first chapter – low, long, with hanging lamps and doors on each side? This is the *Aquitania*'s Alice Gallery, and, that nothing may be missing, a children's nursery lies below, crammed with toys. Down on D-deck there is an information bureau, which lives well up to its name, and a bank, a real live bank, capable of transacting any business. This is the overseas branch of the London Joint City and Midland Bank Ltd.

The *Aquitania* is not a 'floating hotel', any more than a good yacht is a 'floating flat.' Hotels and flats are full of noise and restlessness and are generally overcrowded. The wonder ship is a glorious country house with just the right number of people in it and plenty of room for them all. I have only one complaint to offer her owners. She averages over 22 knots and I can only spend a week at a time aboard her, because she gets there too soon.

Coincidentally, Northcliffe's article was published in 1921, the *Aquitania*'s most popular year. T.E. Hughes' article 'Three Million Ocean Miles', published by *Sea Breezes* magazine in 1950, recalled a regular Cunard traveller who had sailed on all three of their Southampton express ships. In 1922, he had described the *Aquitania* as 'perfection' and said, 'I don't think you will ever beat her … I always engage B100 on the *Aquitania*,

Above, left and right: *Aquitania* sometimes carried unusual cargoes. In these two pictures, an engine crankshaft is loaded on board. Since it has four crank pins, it is intended either for a four-cylinder triple extension engine or a quadruple expansion engine. The photograph appears to have been taken in New York, making this an eastbound cargo. (J. & C. McCutcheon collection)

The competition: in 1937, *Aquitania* was photographed from the decks of a German express liner. (Clyde George collection)

Docked at New York in the late 1930s, many anticipated *Aquitania* would soon be withdrawn from service. (Clyde George collection)

and really I do not think there is a finer suite of rooms in any liner afloat.' Yet Cunard always sought to improve matters, and in the spring of 1923 *Aquitania* was 'completely repainted and redecorated' at a cost of $500,000.

As the times changed, *Aquitania* had to adapt. Although the reduction in third-class travel lowered passenger numbers, from a revenue viewpoint it is something of a myth that third class paid for these large liners. This might have been true for those liners with an enormous third-class capacity and less first-class accommodation, yet with the finest first-class suites costing more than a great many third-class tickets, it does not appear to have been true for *Aquitania*'s ilk. Nevertheless, shipping lines were always seeking to improve their earnings, and in the middle of the decade a new concept was introduced to the North Atlantic routes in the form of 'tourist third cabin.' Passengers travelling in this class paid a little more than normal third-class rates, yet were rewarded with either the superior third- or lower-second-class accommodation. The intention was to attract those who wished to travel in relative comfort without paying a lot of money for the privilege.

While prohibition was in force in America, Ellen Williamson recalls an exciting trip to New York on *Aquitania*. Her family dined with Frank and Clara Kellogg – the British Ambassador and his wife – who invited them to accompany them off the ship and thereby bypass customs. Seizing a chance 'too good to be true', Ellen and her sister Barbara bought 'dozens' of bottles of Scotch and brandy to hide in their luggage. They managed to utilise their mother's standing wardrobe trunk as well. When, safely away, the time came

to unpack, 'mother was astonished and horrified at what she saw, but most amused'.[6]

At the end of 1926, *Aquitania* spent two months in dry dock, with no fewer than 1,500 workmen continuously employed in this thorough refurbishment, and between 2,000 and 3,000 workers at its peak. The 100-ton rudder was removed, examined and reassembled. Five tons of paint were 'chipped from each of her four funnels'. Cargo gear was 'thoroughly overhauled. The great turbine engines have been lifted and cleansed. The machines on which depend the facilities for ventilation, sanitation, cold storage, and pumping have been adjusted and repaired … And all done right to time – another tribute to British industry.'

Cunard told the press that no less than three miles of new carpet had been laid, while '2,000 yards of new damask' had been 'used for wall coverings.' Among the improvements, 'American sun parlours' had reportedly been added to two of the first-class suites. Twenty-four new 'exceptionally large' deluxe suite rooms had been installed on B-deck, by removing a number of ordinary first-class staterooms and 'abolishing the raised part – the chair deck, that is – of the promenade' on the port and starboard sides. Cunard described them in detail:

A variety of polished inlaid hardwoods has been used with gay-coloured carpets and wall fabrics. The decoration schemes also vary, and the work has been in every instance carried out with fine artistic taste. Through large sash windows and not portholes voyagers will look across what is left of these promenade decks to the sea beyond. They are a charming addition to the popular liner's many attractions…

The suites were arranged 'so that two double bedrooms, their bathrooms and a central sitting room can be made into one suite.' Decorated in very different styles, the suites had 'the appearance of spaciousness'.

After 1926, passenger capacities were given as 610 cabin (first) class, 950 in second class, and 640 in tourist (third) class,[7] yet the North Atlantic Passenger Conference listed her as carrying first-, second- and third-class passengers. She sailed from Southampton on 5 January 1927, beginning what would be her busiest year of the 1920s, involving sixteen-and-a-half round trips to New York. She would carry tourist-class passengers for the first time, before their numbers swelled at the end of the decade.

Aside from changing circumstances, storms were a frequent threat to liners' schedules. On 31 December 1924, *Aquitania* arrived in New York with 787 passengers, some thirty hours late after a westbound passage that was her longest to date. Captain Charles explained that from Thursday morning 'until Sunday afternoon one gale followed another, with hurricanes in between. The seas were terrific. Two waves came over the bridge at 8 o'clock on Friday night

Capt. E. G. Diggle, R.D., R.N.R., *Saxonia*.   Capt. H. M. Benison, R.N.R., *Ivernia*.   Capt. W. Prothero, *Carpathia*.

Capt. G. W. Melsom, R.N.R., *Ascania*.   Capt. S. G. S. McNeil, R.D., R.N.R., *Ausonia*.

Capt. R. Capper, R.N.R., *Pannonia*.   Capt. R. G. Malin, R.N.R., *Ultonia*.

Capt. J. T. W. Charles, C.B., R.D., R.N.R., *Lusitania*.   Capt. J. C. Barr (Commodore), *Carmania*.   Capt. W. T. Turner, R.N.R., *Mauretania*.

Capt. C. A. Smith, R.D., R.N.R., *Franconia*.   Capt. D. Dow, R.D., R.N.R., *Caronia*.

Capt. D. S. Miller, R.D., R.N.R., *Andania*.   Capt. W. R. D. Irvine, R.D., R.N.R., *Laconia*.   Capt. A. H. Rostron, R.D., R.N.R., *Campania*.

Above: By the late 1930s, many anticipated that *Aquitania* would soon be withdrawn from service, yet time after time she continued a hectic schedule of round trips. Here, she is shown leaving New York after yet another turnaround. (J. & C. McCutcheon collection)

Left and far left: Cunard's captains. Seen here prior to the war, many would go on to command *Aquitania*. (Mike Poirier collection)

and smashed two of the windows on the starboard side and two of the small upper windows along the B-deck forward.' *Aquitania*'s speed had been reduced to 9 knots for forty-eight hours, covering only 220 miles on her worst day's run. Docking was delayed two hours by ice flows when she arrived in New York on 17 February 1926, following an eighteen-hour delay due to bad weather. At 7 p.m. one evening, as the sea conditions improved, speed was increased from 10 to 15 knots, yet as passengers entered the dining room a 60ft wave hit, smashing a 'heavy steel girder on the forward deck amidships' and carrying away a cargo derrick. When it reached the bridge, the wave hit the chart room, smashing two windows on the port side, while the letter 'Q' was missing from the ship's name on the bow. Captain Charles reduced speed to 8 knots for two hours, while the only trace of the girder was a 1ft stump on the deck where it had been snapped off and carried overboard. The harsh Atlantic was unforgiving.

For Cunard, and not least *Aquitania*'s passengers and crew, 15 July 1928 was a sad day. Commodore Sir James Charles had almost completed his final voyage, having commanded *Aquitania* since March 1918, and 'after an exceptionally good' crossing he handed over to the pilot at Cherbourg. Ten minutes later, the bell from his cabin rang and officers found he had collapsed. Two doctors diagnosed a 'severe internal haemorrhage' and he was semi-conscious on the return to Southampton, but he died shortly after being taken ashore 'without fully regaining consciousness.' Newspapers reported that he had told passengers 'that he had not realised until then how difficult it was to part from his old shipmates.' Charles had crossed the Atlantic no fewer than 726 times, and his friend Captain Sir Arthur Rostron (later Commodore) told reporters:

Commodore Sir James Charles was a man we all admired and all had a great affection for. His manly courtesy and thoughtful kindness was manifested in so many and varied ways. As a distinguished seaman, he was known and admired by everyone. He leaves hosts of friends who will always think of him as a good friend, a splendid and interesting shipmate and an example to the rising generation of officers.

Ellen Williamson recalled meeting Charles several years earlier, writing:

He was one of the largest men I've ever seen in my life and one of the handsomest. At the Captain's dinner (always the next-to-the-last night before landing) he had the most gold braid on his uniform and the most ribbons (for medals) that I ever saw on any one person. He came over to our table and shook hands with all of us, and told sister Barbara and me that we were going to enjoy excessively the special dessert of the evening. And we did: it was a soufflé served by a chef in a two-foot-high chef's hat, and the soufflé was the same height and surrounded by glacéed strawberries and pink spun sugar.[8]

There was some excitement when *Aquitania* arrived in New York twenty-four hours late on 1 December 1928, delayed due to rough weather and an aborted rescue attempt with the *Admiral Ponty*. Captain William Prothero explained that, 'At 8 a.m. Sunday [25 November 1928], while passing Bishop's Rock, we picked up the first SOS, and I steamed full speed to her assistance. At 10 o'clock I radioed the master if he wished to abandon the ship, and he replied: "No, we do not intend to abandon the ship."' With the French freighter *Macrois* standing by, *Aquitania* resumed her course, although with a gale blowing and heavy seas the weather was by no means perfect. By 12 p.m., another SOS was received as the *Admiral Ponty*'s No. 1 hold was filling and her pumps had stopped operating. Prothero was forced to alter course again and reached the sinking ship at 3 p.m. However, heavy seas hampered matters and it was difficult to distinguish between the two vessels. While *Aquitania*'s lifeboats were readied for a rescue attempt, the weather moderated and the French vessel took over the rescue.

Aquitania underwent an extensive, five-week refit at the start of 1929. In a brochure issued in January 1929, Cunard said that a 'tremendous amount of work was accomplished during her systematic overhaul, in the course of which over 1,000 workmen of all trades were continuously employed.' Thousands of gallons of paint were used in refreshing the ship's hull, decks, funnels and superstructure, while hundreds of square yards of new carpet had been laid, and various curtains and hangings changed.

First class now enjoyed a new 'American bar' constructed just off the long gallery, designed with a vellum-coloured ceiling and grey oak panelling. The bar itself was 'a long counter with a brass foot rail, round which are grouped stools, covered with ruboleum in a pleasing design of grey squares with joints of bright blue.' Cunard claimed that it expressed the popular 'modern movement in decoration which was launched with great éclat at the Paris Exhibition of 1925.' In the first-class companionways and staircases, 'an entirely new design of Sienna marble tiling' had been installed, consisting of enlarged panels of blue and stone. The Adam-style writing room, Elizabethan grill room and Carolean smoking room were cleaned to look 'more impressive than ever.' Not content to rest, Cunard decided to redecorate many of the first-class rooms on A-, B- and C-decks. Meanwhile, on C-deck many of the first-class rooms fitted with private toilets had been renovated: 'The private bathrooms and showers, with their blue and white marble mosaic floors, are equipped with the very latest fittings, and throughout the ship particular attention has been paid to the lighting and water supply.'

In second class, the drawing room had been completely 'redecorated in new biscuit colourings with ivory enrichment,' with a new carpet being fitted. The dining room chairs had been 're-covered with French woven panel tapestries, with a blue ground.' The second-class veranda café had been fitted with new wicker furniture and everywhere, carpets, curtains and furniture had been cleaned and polished.

Cunard were proud of the new tourist accommodation as well, stating: 'In one section of the ship the accommodation has been completely remodelled, providing no less than four new public rooms, new staterooms and promenade space for the new class known as tourist third cabin.' One of the company's publicity statements described the new areas in great detail:

… Thousands of pounds have been spent in providing an entirely new range of public rooms, consisting of [a] smoking room, lounge, dining saloon, and a winter garden. In addition, a whole range of comfortable staterooms has been provided on two decks. There is also a large amount of promenade space specially set aside for this class. This new accommodation should certainly prove a great attraction to the holiday maker wishing to travel to the United States in a mammoth Cunarder in comfort, but at a reasonably low rate.

The new smoking room, which is situated on C-deck, is decorated to represent a half-timbered room with oak beams. The floors are treated with a flagstone design of ruboleum, and the furniture consists of tub and easy chairs, covered in stretched hide, and a number of old-fashioned Windsor wheel-back chairs reminiscent of an old farm house. The dining saloon, which is on D-deck, is large enough to accommodate 200 people at a single sitting, small tables to set four or six persons being provided. Brown, yellow and green are the colours employed in the bright semi-modern cretonnes of the tourist third cabin lounge, which has a large number of comfortable easy chairs with attractive loose covers, as well as brightly-coloured wicker chairs in orange and green. The new staterooms look very inviting with their gleaming white enamelled walls, red Wilton rugs, and up-to-date electric light fittings of the latest shell pattern. New ruboleum has been laid throughout the new tourist third [class] accommodation.

The 'new' *Aquitania* had emerged even more impressive, and on leaving Southampton for her first round trip to New York, 'The 900 foot long vessel appeared imposingly beautiful when she began to sheer off from the Quayside; and nothing could be more impressive than the picture she presented as, gathering way, her formidable bulk glided out of the placid waters of the dock with the gracefulness of a swan. The sun glistened with dazzling effect on the flamboyant red of the four enormous funnels – so enormous that no less than five tons of old paint had been chipped off each.'

Certainly, the new 'tourist third cabin' accommodation appeared popular. *Aquitania* had first carried 'tourist third cabin' passengers in 1927, carrying 295 passengers that year and 517 passengers in 1928 (all westbound). Yet in 1929 she carried 4,329 tourist-third-class passengers, a similar number in each direction. Numbers rose to 5,073 in 1930, and 5,798 on a busy year in 1931.[9] Cunard had successfully adapted her to cope with the changing competitive situation on the Atlantic. Even as times changed, all of Cunard's three ships earned impressive profits. *Aquitania* logged a profit of £488,438 in 1926, £746,044 in 1927, £708,516 in 1928, and £662,641 in 1929.[10]

Yet change was afoot for Cunard's express service. Increasing competition signalled that plans needed to be developed to replace their three large express ships. In the late 1920s, Cunard were planning ahead for two new large liners to operate their express service for the following decade. These liners eventually became the *Queen Mary* and *Queen Elizabeth*. Once the first liner's construction began, Cunard ultimately decided on building the second, although in March 1930 Cunard's naval architect believed 'it was quite possible on economic grounds the decision would be in favour of reconditioning and re-engining the *Aquitania*, although he personally was in favour of another big [new] liner.' Even the first new liner's construction came into question following the Wall Street Crash of 1929.

After fifteen years in service, *Aquitania* was performing well, yet with the onset of the Great Depression many shipping companies would find it a struggle to stay in business. Competition was intensifying, as passenger lists fell and the older liners began to show signs of age. Tough times lay ahead.

NOTES

1 Spedding, page 166.

2 op. cit., page 192.

3 op. cit., pages 166–67.

4 op. cit., page 172.

5 op. cit., pages 172–73.

6 Williamson, pages 137–38.

7 *Engineering* Special, page vii.

8 Williamson, pages 120–21.

9 *Aquitania* is listed as carrying both second- and tourist cabin passengers from 1927 to 1931, yet from 1932 onwards no second-class passengers are listed, only tourist cabin passengers being carried alongside first class and third class.

10 For a detailed comparison table, see the appendices.

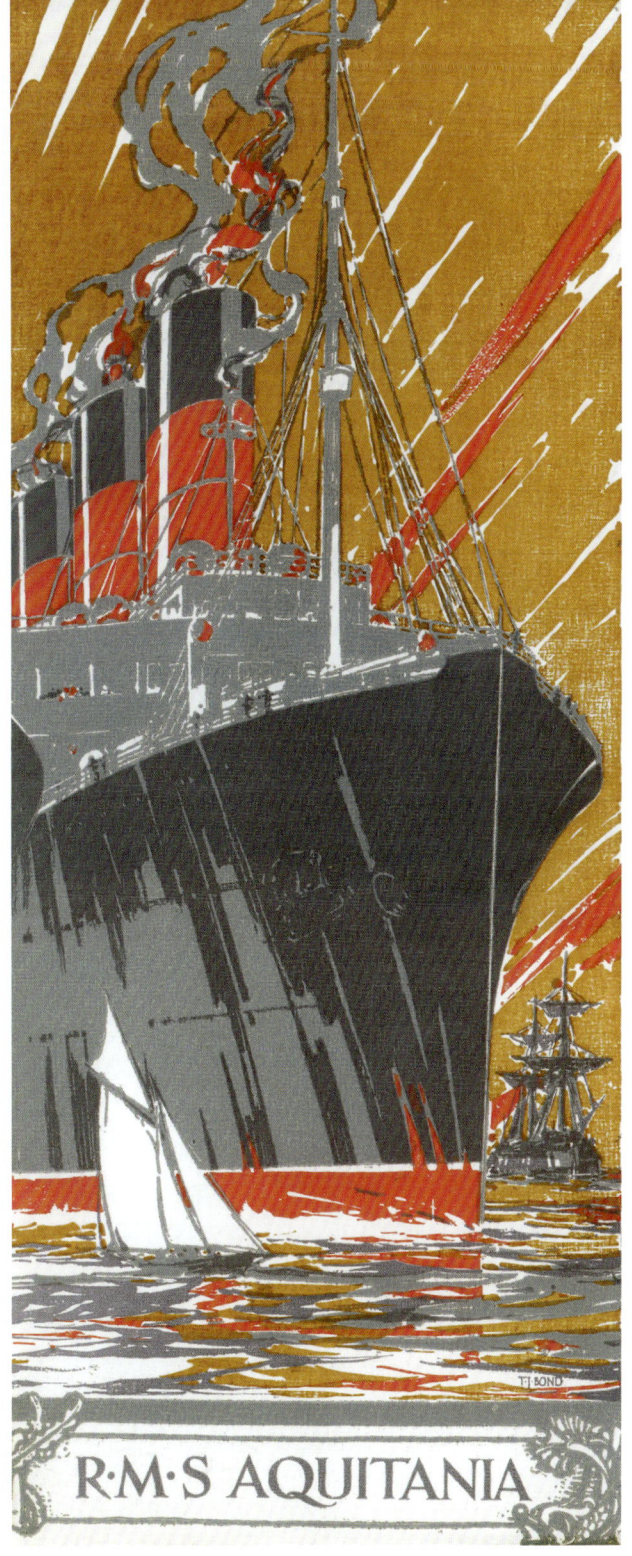

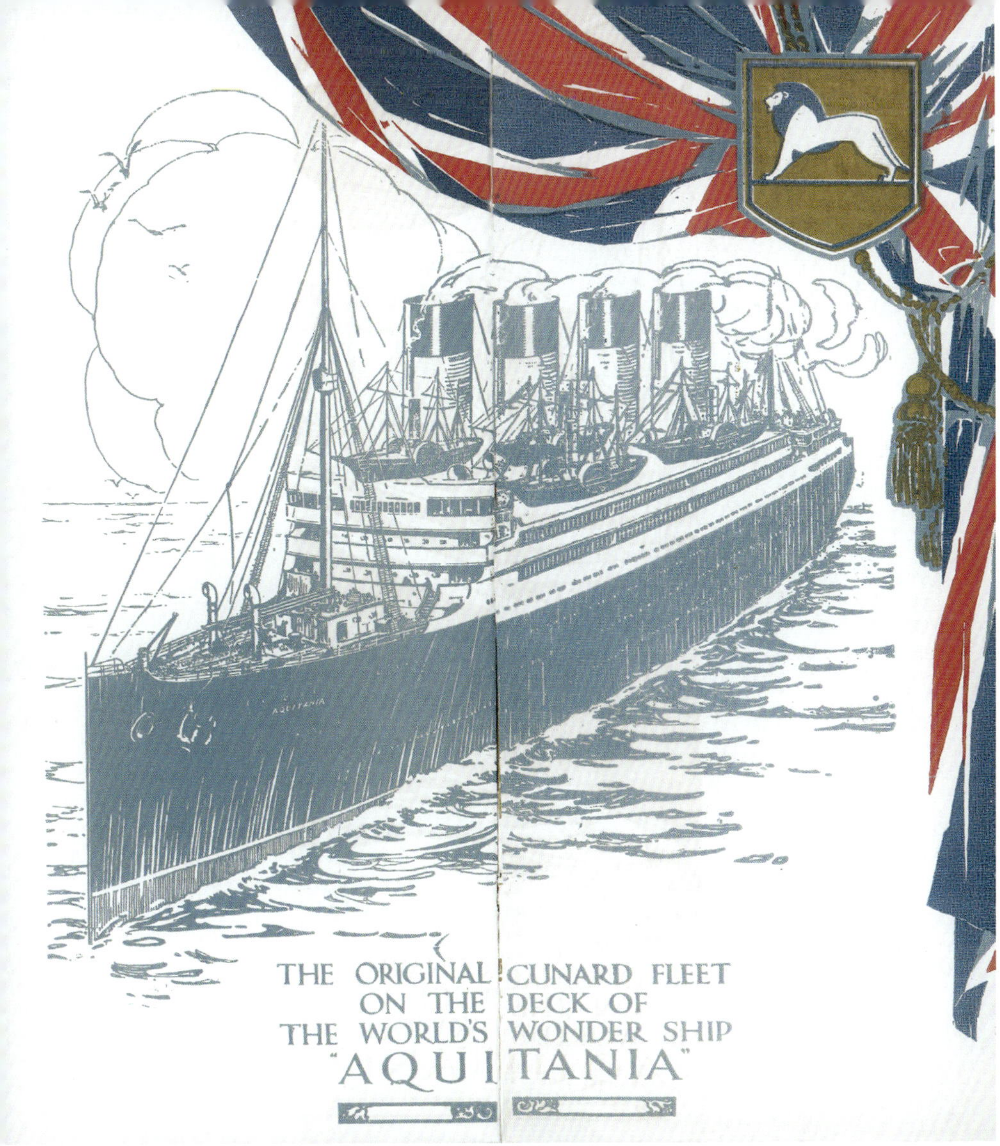
THE ORIGINAL CUNARD FLEET
ON THE DECK OF
THE WORLD'S WONDER SHIP
"AQUITANIA"

Above: 'Eight decades of progress' – a lovely view of *Aquitania* produced for the British Empire Exhibition at Wembley, 1924. (J. & C. McCutcheon collection)

Right: RMS *Aquitania*. (J. & C. McCutcheon collection)

T.J. BOND
R·M·S AQUITANIA

Above: A lovely view of *Aquitania* arriving in New York, in which the liner's height appears to compare favourably with the city buildings. (Clyde George collection)

Right: One of Cunard's stylish brochures advertising third-class accommodation, which was issued around 1929.

Far right: Cunard ensure that *Aquitania* is associated with the company by displaying the name and famous Lion. (Clyde George collection)

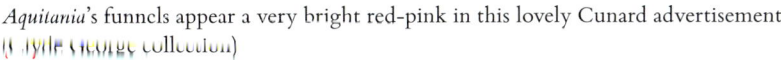

Aquitania's funnels appear a very bright red-pink in this lovely Cunard advertisement. (Clyde George collection)

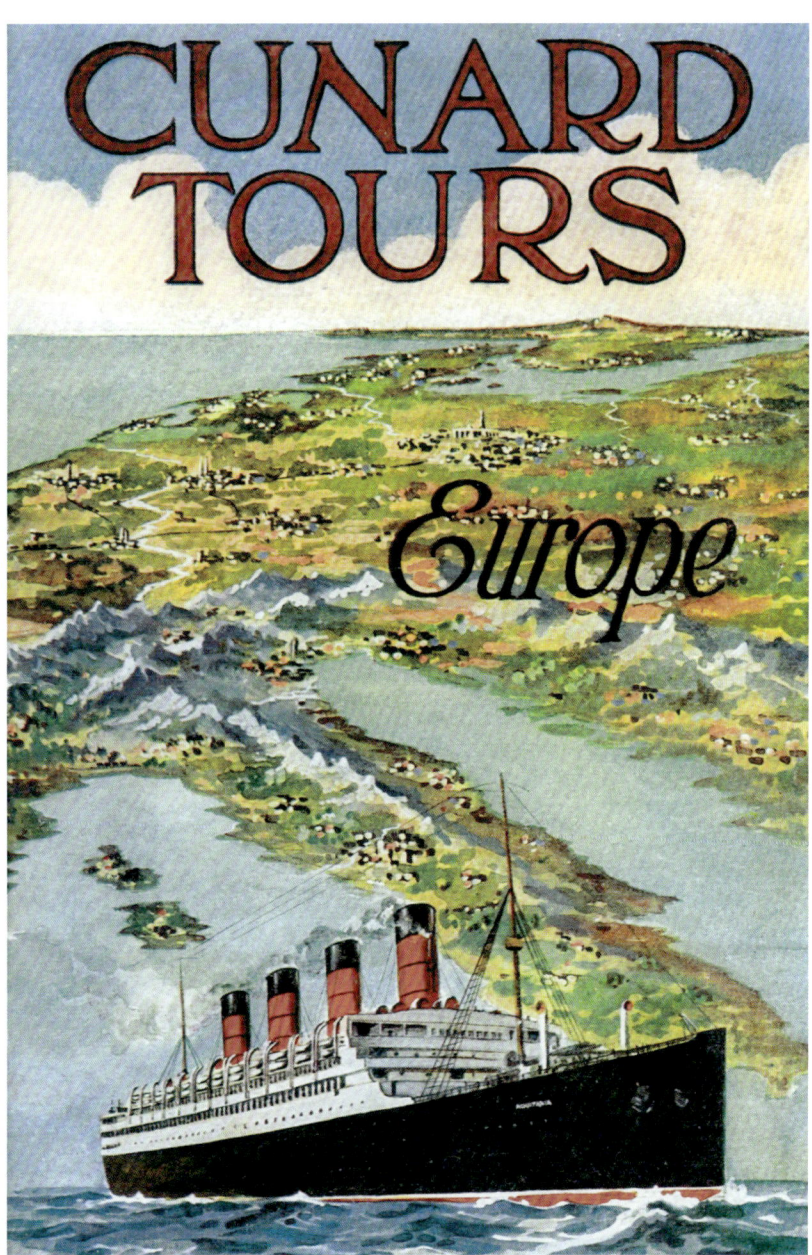

Advertising tours to Europe. (Clyde George collection)

Above: A fantastic view of *Aquitania* compared to the tiny tugs. The blast of steam from the forward funnel and the deep red colour of the 'smokestacks' bring to mind an atmosphere of character-full steamships. (Author's collection)

Above left: Sometimes called Cunard's 'Big Three' – *Mauretania*, *Aquitania* and *Berengaria* in a wonderfully evocative image from the early 1920s.
(J. & C. McCutcheon collection)

Centre left: Steamship companies were often eager to inform travellers of their liners' sterling service during the First World War. Here, *Aquitania* is shown as a hospital ship. The wonderful colouring is particularly evident by looking at the sky. (J. & C. McCutcheon collection)

Below left: Rust-streaked, *Aquitania* is shown as a troopship with 'dazzle' paint scheme, ploughing through some rather choppy seas.
(Clyde George collection)

Above: Although aged, this is a wonderful scene. Identified merely as a 'Cunarder at Southampton', it is obviously *Aquitania*. (Author's collection)

Left: A lovely image created by John Fry in 1922. His style is evident when comparing the bow wave with his 1923 image of *Majestic* (*RMS Majestic: The 'Magic Stick'*).

Cunard Line

R.M.S. "Aquitania."

LENGTH 901 FEET – BREADTH 97 FEET – DEPTH (from Boat Deck) 92½ FEET – GROSS TONNAGE 47,000 – SPEED 23

Above: Cunard issued a cutaway profile of *Aquitania* after she had been converted to oil fuel. They exaggerated her gross tonnage, giving the figure as 47,000 tons. (Author's collection)

Lunch on board *Aquitania* as the war drew to a close. The food was not as varied as that of the pre- or post-war years, although it was wholesome. (Mike Poirier collection)

Just over a year later, peace had returned. (Mike Poirier collection)

GHT TO TOPS OF FUNNELS 164 FEET—HEIGHT TO MASTHEADS 220 FEET—ACCOMMODATION FOR NEARLY 5,000.

Cunard's pride on the front of a brochure for first- and second-class passengers, issued in the early 1920s. (Author's collection)

A lovely decorative cover for a first-class menu presented to ex-President William Taft and his wife on 7 November 1923. (Author's collection)

Specially arranged Tours in Canada and U.S.A

IT is difficult to imagine a more thrilling and enjoyable holiday than a **6,000** miles cruise across the Atlantic in a giant modern Cunard liner. Apart from the wonderfully bracing effect of the voyage itself, such a holiday affords a complete escape from the routine and restrictions of a more conventional holiday at home. Everything is carefully thought out for your comfort and entertainment, and from the moment you embark you will have a delicious sense of freedom, a feeling that time-tables, baggage, hotel accommodation and other worries of a holiday ashore can be banished utterly from your mind.

Trips to New York — Niagara Falls & the Great Chicago Exhibition

THEN there is the immense interest of exploring for yourself some of the wonders of the United States and Canada—New York with its fantastic skyline of towering skyscrapers, vastly populated industrial centres contrasted with wide fertile plains and prairies, the stately Capitol at Washington and old-world Quebec, the thundering cascades of Niagara Falls. An additional attraction this year is the wonderful Century of Progress Exhibition on the lake front at Chicago with its spectacular effects in illumination, ultra-modern experiments in architecture, and unlimited opportunities for recreation and amusement.

Cunard

Cunard

Gorgeous illustrations of *Aquitania* were issued in this 1930s brochure. (Author's collection)

An *Aquitania* baggage tag. (Author's collection)

Above: A fine image dating from the 1930s. (Author's collection)

Right: Another Turner scene, showing *Aquitania*'s vast bulk. (J. & C. McCutcheon collection)

five

THE SPRIGHTLY LADY

*A*quitania continued to be popular after the onset of the Depression. In 1931, she was behind only the new *Bremen* and *Europa* in terms of the total number of passengers carried, and ahead of the fashionable *Ile de France*.[1] Her solid tourist-class passenger lists helped her and the completion of eighteen round trips that year was remarkable. Even so, all liners began to suffer. Her average passenger lists showed a general decline from 872 passengers per crossing in 1930 to 464 passengers in 1933.

Cunard turned to cruising as an additional source of revenue, and as well as her tiring service on the express route in 1931, *Aquitania* made a number of cruises, including four-day cruises from New York. Early in April 1931, Cunard announced the plans and before its offices had closed that day, more than 200 passengers had been booked for the *Aquitania*'s first cruising voyage. For a minimum of $50 (and a maximum of $100), passengers could join *Aquitania* for her departure from New York at 10 a.m. on 2 May, heading out to the Gulf Stream and then returning to New York by 5 p.m. on 5 May. *Mauretania*'s cruises had proved very popular and Cunard wanted to maximise the opportunities available. It was estimated that between 650 and 800 passengers could be attracted for each cruise. Only first and second class were open, with a 'first class service' and all passengers were granted access to the ship's amenities regardless of the price of their ticket. On her early July 1931 weekend cruise to Halifax, *Aquitania*'s passenger list was 1,170, far more than might have been expected on the Atlantic run. Things were not so rosy in December 1931, when one planned cruise had to be cancelled through lack of interest.

Many vessels began to run at a loss as the occasional drop of red ink turned into a flood. Passenger lists fell markedly. Page after page in ledger books were written almost entirely in red. Westbound crossings in September were always great for lengthy passenger lists, yet even here there was bad news. Leaving Southampton on 31 August 1929, *Aquitania*'s round trip to New York brought a gross profit of almost £68,000; on her 30 August 1930 round trip she recorded a profit of £58,071; then on her 10 September 1932 round trip she was in the black by £29,228; but by her 1 September 1934 round trip she made a gross profit of £9,677, which was actually a tiny net loss of £73. On many voyages throughout the year, liners began to run at a loss even before depreciation and other expenses were taken into account. Falling passenger lists were not the only problem to be dealt with, for fares were being reduced as well. On 23 July 1931, the *New York Times* printed a letter from a Mr Otto A.C. Hagan of Philadelphia, who was 'pleased to see that the drastic decline in first class patronage has finally alarmed the Atlantic lines'. He blamed high fares, arguing that prices should be reduced considerably and 'as travel increases, so will the earnings, and after all that is what the lines are in business for'. He pointed to the good passenger lists seen on cruises where the fares were low. Cunard was reducing fares too, yet the simple truth was that supply far outstripped demand and passenger lists continued to fall.

The situation looked particularly bleak for the older liners, for as passenger numbers fell an increasing proportion booked on newer express ships. In 1929, Nordeutscher Lloyd's *Bremen* won the Blue Riband on her maiden voyage, and carried 24,960 passengers that year compared to *Mauretania*'s 18,842. A stark reality was illustrated by the fact that *Bremen* had carried more passengers even though she had only been in service since July. By 1931, Cunard's express trio were carrying a total of 47,960 passengers, which was little more than *Bremen*'s newer sister *Europa* had carried on her own! In December 1932, Lord Weir endorsed Cunard's plan for two new, large express liners capable of providing

Originally placed on the Board of Trade's Confidential List owing to repairs to her stern frame and rudder, *Aquitania* began to show signs of weakness towards the bow. In March 1924, two fractures were noted near two portholes between E- and F-decks, and slack rivets were noted in 1925, 1928 and 1929. In April 1931, a fracture near another porthole close by needed repairing. During her annual survey in November 1933, the shell plating had fractured over 12in beneath 'the lower after corner of the forward gangway [door] opening immediately below the break of the bridge' on both the port and starboard sides. To make matters worse, a large fracture on the port side (about 30in long) was discovered 'through the sheer stake and the doubling.' The fractured plating near the gangways was replaced; for additional strength, the affected gangway doors on each side were permanently removed and plated over. (After the similar fracture on the starboard side continued to extend in the mid-1940s, further 'substantial' repairs were undertaken in 1948.) Looking back to her grounding in the Mersey, one of the Board of Trade surveyors had 'no doubt the vessel was badly strained in the vicinity of the break of the bridge forward'. Whether the grounding exacerbated an existing problem or created a potential weakness to surface years after is a matter for debate. Although every care had been taken with the ship's design, practical experience demonstrated the reality of shipbuilding as a progressive science. *Aquitania*'s long years of hard service showed the fundamental strength of her construction. (Courtesy of the National Archives)

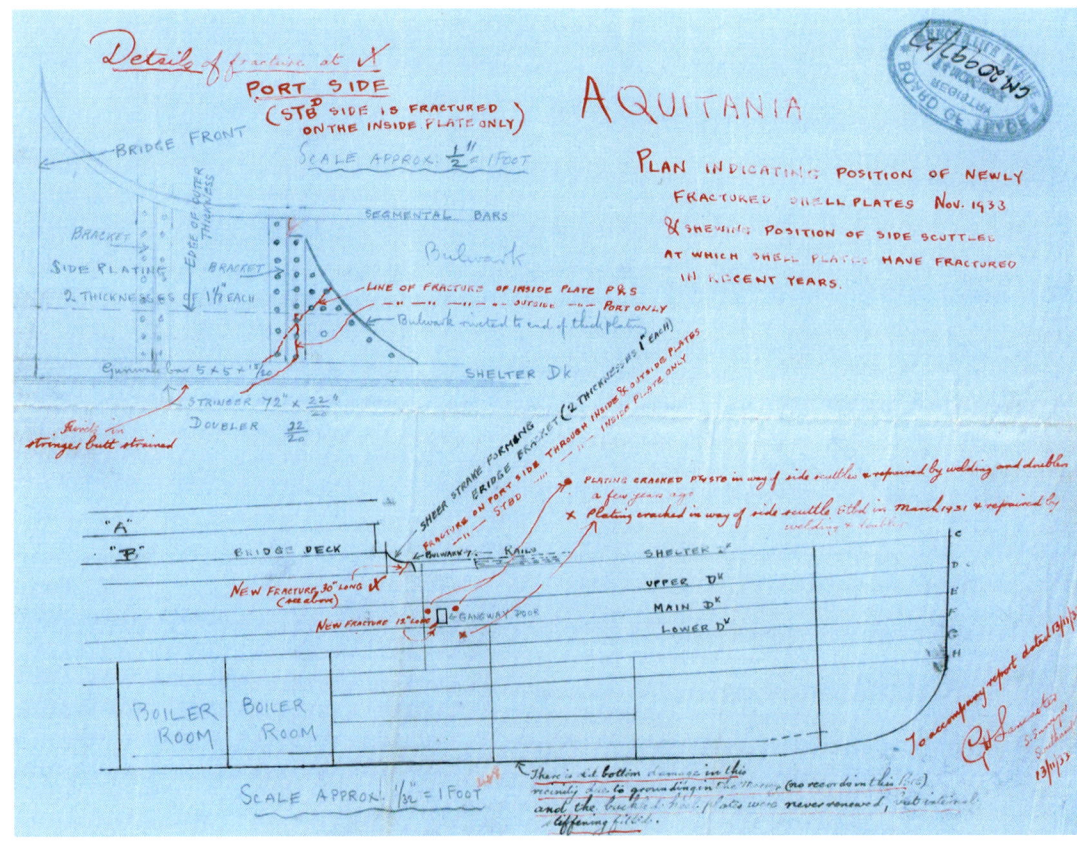

A grand sight! (Clyde George collection)

Unlike some of her rivals, all *Aquitania*'s funnels were fully functioning. (Clyde George collection)

a weekly service, saying that even 'three modern vessels of the *Aquitania* type would neither meet the competition nor yield the same economic return.' He pointed out that technology had improved markedly – *Berengaria* required 9,400 tons of oil for a round trip at 24 knots, but the new 'No.534' [*Queen Mary*] would only need 10,100 tons for the same voyage at 28.5 knots.

If there was faith that new tonnage could turn the situation around, Cunard were, for the time, being caught in a trap. Economic circumstances forced construction of the new No.534 to be suspended before the end of 1931. It was only through the merger of Cunard and White Star, agreed at the end of 1933 and effective by summer 1934, that construction would resume.

By 1932, *Aquitania*'s schedule included eleven round trips to New York, yet late in January 1932 Cunard announced that two thirty-day cruises would go ahead on 3 February 1932 and 5 March 1932, including a call at Port Said, Egypt, followed by a day's stop on the homeward voyage at the Aegean island of Rhodes. Cunard were confident that enough bookings had been made to justify them. It was a busy year on the Atlantic for the *Aquitania*, as she also made several shorter cruises, and in 1933 she would make fifteen round trips to New York. *Aquitania* underwent a lengthy refit towards the end of 1932 and Cunard lost no time in publicising the improvements the following year.

Aquitania's first voyage following the refit was beset by bad weather, and she docked twelve hours late, at 11.15 p.m. on 10 January 1933. She was the first ship to dock at Cunard's new Pier 54, as the old pier had been destroyed by fire in the spring of 1932. 10,000 sacks of mail were on board, while there was a hurried turnaround since she was due to depart for Southampton at 10.30 p.m. the following day. The *New York Times* carried a report about the refit:

Left: Even the grime of an industrial port fails to take the shine off *Aquitania*. (Author's collection)

Below: Aquitania's profile projected an image of power and strength that was entirely accurate. After twenty-five years in service, her performance compared favourably with *Lusitania*'s and *Mauretania*'s early voyages, as she regularly logged a day's run well in excess of 25 knots. (Clyde George collection)

Above left: Another image romanticising *Aquitania*. (Clyde George collection)

Above right: Even allowing for *Aquitania*'s height being exaggerated in this illustration, the tugs appear extremely small alongside. An eagle eye might spot that the ship appears out of proportion to her true length and breadth. (Clyde George collection)

THE CUNARDER
AQUITANIA

Above: Published in the 1930s, an illustration by artist Fred J. Moeratz shows its age. (Clyde George collection)

Left: Leaving port, the curve of the bow is more extreme than in reality, while – as usual – the tugs appear far too small in comparison. (Clyde George collection)

AQUITANIA TOURIST CLASS

IF BY some romantic chance you were to fall asleep and suddenly wake up aboard the Aquitania (familiarly known as the wonder ship of the Atlantic) travelling to Europe in her Tourist Class, you'd probably think you were in a great English mansion done in the Grand Manner. One reason for the surprising quality of Tourist Class is that, not so long ago, some of the staterooms were First Class and the remainder comprised Second Cabin accommodations. An-

Cunard extolled the benefits of tourist class in this 17 April 1935 brochure text. (Author's collection)

Right above: In tourist class on Sunday 15 August 1937, two golden fish were used on the dinner menu's centrepiece. Near the bottom, a three-funnelled liner was presumably the new *Queen Mary*. While passengers enjoyed less choice than their first-class counterparts, the menu was plentiful and included options 'from the grill'. (Author's collection)

Right below: *Aquitania* is depicted on the front of a prayer card sent to passengers who were at sea during the festive season. Remarkably, the liner shown is actually the White Star Line's *Olympic*, as she appeared in publicity material issued early in her career! The white-painted plating beneath the forecastle, among other features, gives the game away, although the funnels are shown in Cunard colours. (Clyde George collection)

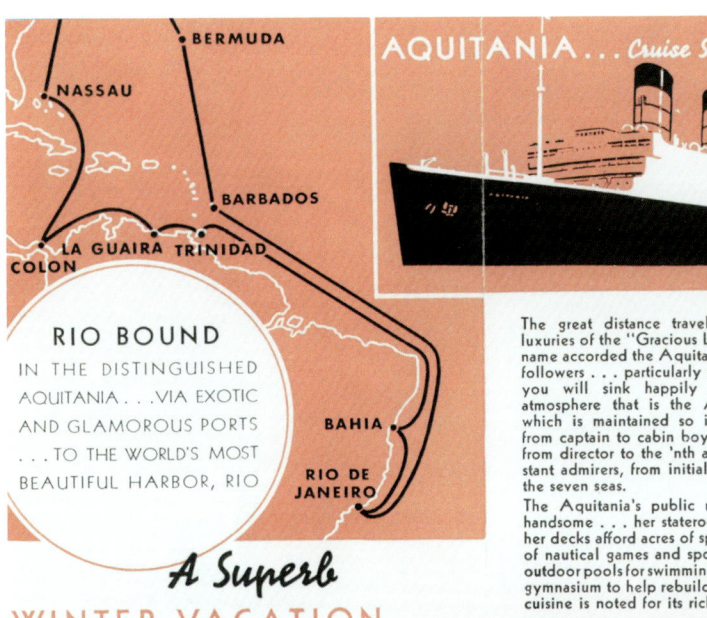

AQUITANIA... *Cruise Ship par Excellence*

RIO BOUND

IN THE DISTINGUISHED AQUITANIA...VIA EXOTIC AND GLAMOROUS PORTS ...TO THE WORLD'S MOST BEAUTIFUL HARBOR, RIO

A Superb

WINTER VACATION

South America in 1938 CAN be yours — is AGAIN yours — in the Aquitania. Covering a distance of nearly 12,000 miles, the equivalent of approximately two transatlantic round trips, the cruise stops at more different ports than any other cruise of similar length — 8 "high-spot" ports in South America, the West Indies, Central America, Bahamas and Bermuda. Though only 33 days duration, more than the ordinary length of time is provided in ports of call because of the speed of the Aquitania — for many years Flagship of the Cunard White Star Fleet.

CUNARD WHITE STAR

The great distance travelled makes the special luxuries of the "Gracious Lady of the Sea"... the name accorded the Aquitania by a host of devoted followers ... particularly desirable. Therefore ... you will sink happily into the soul-warming atmosphere that is the Aquitania's, alone, and which is maintained so insistently by her crew, from captain to cabin boy ... by her cruise staff, from director to the 'nth assistant ... by her constant admirers, from initial voyagers to veterans of the seven seas.

The Aquitania's public rooms are spacious and handsome ... her staterooms unusually large ... her decks afford acres of space for the whole gamut of nautical games and sports ... plus indoor and outdoor pools for swimming ... and a well equipped gymnasium to help rebuild flagging muscles ... her cuisine is noted for its richness and variety.

⚓ **ITINERARY** ⚓

	Miles	Arrival		Departure	
New York.....	.....	.....		Thur.	Feb. 17 Noon
Nassau......	961	Sat.	Feb. 19 a.m.	Sun.	Feb. 20 2a.m.
Colon......	1162	Tues.	Feb. 22 a.m.	Wed.	Feb. 23 6p.m.
La Guaira....	834	Fri.	Feb. 25 a.m.	Fri.	Feb. 25 6p.m.
Trinidad.....	329	Sat.	Feb. 26 a.m.	Sun.	Feb. 27 Noon
Bahia.......	2450	Fri.	Mar. 4 a.m.	Fri.	Mar. 4 6p.m.
Rio de Janeiro	747	Sun.	Mar. 6 a.m.	Thur.	Mar. 10 5p.m.
Barbados....	3081	Wed.	Mar. 16 Noon	Thur.	Mar. 17 6p.m.
Bermuda.....	1204	Sun.	Mar. 20 a.m.	Sun.	Mar. 20 6p.m.
New York...	693	Tues.	Mar. 22 a.m.		.....
	11,461				

8 "HIGHSPOT" PORTS OF CALL

Nassau, glamorous, gay ... rendezvous of sophisticates ... tropical, with its manner still brilliantly British ... jewel-like, in blue Bahamian seas. Your day and night here will be restful, zestful ...fortifying that shipboard tan on Paradise Beach.

Now, we enter the true melting pot of this hemisphere ... where peoples of all colors and languages are to be found in a setting of tropical splendor and man-made wonders ... the crossroads of the world, the Isthmus of Panama.

Then through the very heart of the old Spanish Main ... to La Guaira in Venezuela. Here rise, like a mighty stage backdrop, the majestic Andes, and up in the mountains is one of the smallest, yet brightest of South American capitals, Caracas.

Now on across the Caribbean to Trinidad ... where black-faced comedians greet the ship in small boats, singing their weird "Calypso" music. You will visit the Mohammedan mosque, the Indian temple ... marvel at the riotous color of jungles.

Foretaste of the fetes and acclaim in Brazil will be the traditional ceremony upon crossing the Equator ... Neptune's Court. First below the line is Bahia former capital of Brazil. The splendor of its 17th century civilization is still a wonder to behold.

No imagination can prepare you for the breath-taking, dazzling loveliness of this silver-white city ... its fantastic background of mountains ... palatial homes, pastel villas ... exuberant, gay, gracious, inviting, warm-hearted Rio.

Barbados is not just a visit ... it's an experience! Rolling plantations of sugar cane (whence molasses, whence rum), surprising windmills ... countless blacks and whites ... concocting rum-swizzles ... perpetuating jazz born of negro rhythm.

Finally Bermuda's pastoral tranquility ... tropical ... full of modern verve and social swing ... yet reminiscent of sleepy English countryside. You relax on sun-warmed sands ... revel in the myriad thoughts of cruise highlights to live forever.

Aquitania was described as a 'cruise ship par excellence' when this brochure was issued for her South American cruises in 1938. (Author's collection)

During the fifty-five day lie-up in Southampton, the interior … was thoroughly overhauled and renovated at a cost of $250,000, to meet the competition of vessels owned by rival companies. Among the noticeable improvements in the first class accommodation is the introduction of more than fifty-five new outside cabins and bathrooms on the A-, B- and C-decks. The large windows on the A- and B-decks open on to the promenade deck and those on the C-deck look out over the ocean. All these spacious rooms have been fitted out with new furniture and rugs, as have many of the other cabins. The Louis XVI restaurant and the Palladian Lounge have also been redecorated and refurnished. The former second class dining room aft on the D-deck has been converted into a theatre, with a stage which occupied three hundred square feet, and two 'green rooms' at the rear.

Seating accommodation is provided by special folding cinema armchairs, which can be quickly removed to make room for dancing. The work of renovation has also been carried out in the tourist and third class accommodations, both in the cabins and the public rooms. An attractive American bar has been installed in the tourist smoking room. The whole ship looked bright and gay last night under the brilliant electric light and the alterations and innovations were admired by the travellers who arrived on the ship.

First-class capacity was generally given as 650 after the refit, while tourist class accommodated 600 passengers and third class 950 passengers.[2] Fortunately, *Aquitania*'s passenger lists began to rise from 1934. She departed Southampton on

AQUITANIA
CRUISE PLAN and RATE SCHEDULE

1938 CRUISE TO THE WEST INDIES AND SOUTH AMERICA

NASSAU, BAHAMAS · COLON, PANAMA · LA GUAIRA, VENEZUELA · BRIDGETOWN, BARBADOS · BAHIA & RIO DE JANEIRO, BRAZIL · PORT-OF-SPAIN, TRINIDAD · ST. GEORGE'S, BERMUDA

from New York
February 17, 1938
NO PASSPORTS REQUIRED
CUNARD WHITE STAR

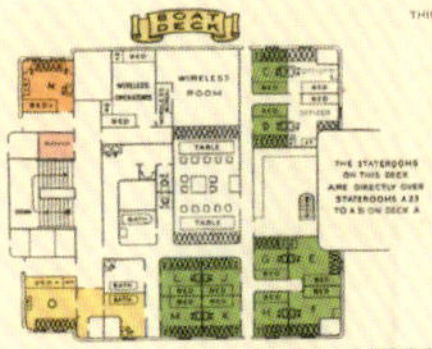

CUNARD WHITE STAR
S. S. AQUITANIA

LENGTH 902 FEET   BREADTH 97 FEET
53,176 TONS DISPLACEMENT   45,647 TONS GROSS

THIRD FOLD   FIRST FOLD   FOURTH FOLD   SECOND FOLD

LIMITED CRUISE MEMBERSHIP

In order to insure comfort on board ship and for shore arrangements, the membership of the cruise will be strictly limited to only a portion of the number for which the *Aquitania* can provide accommodation. Staterooms are arranged for one or two passengers only, since three friends or a family party will share the same cabin. A large number of spacious cabins have been reserved in single rooms, the *Aquitania* is also equipped with an unusually large number of de luxe rooms with private baths and many private suites.

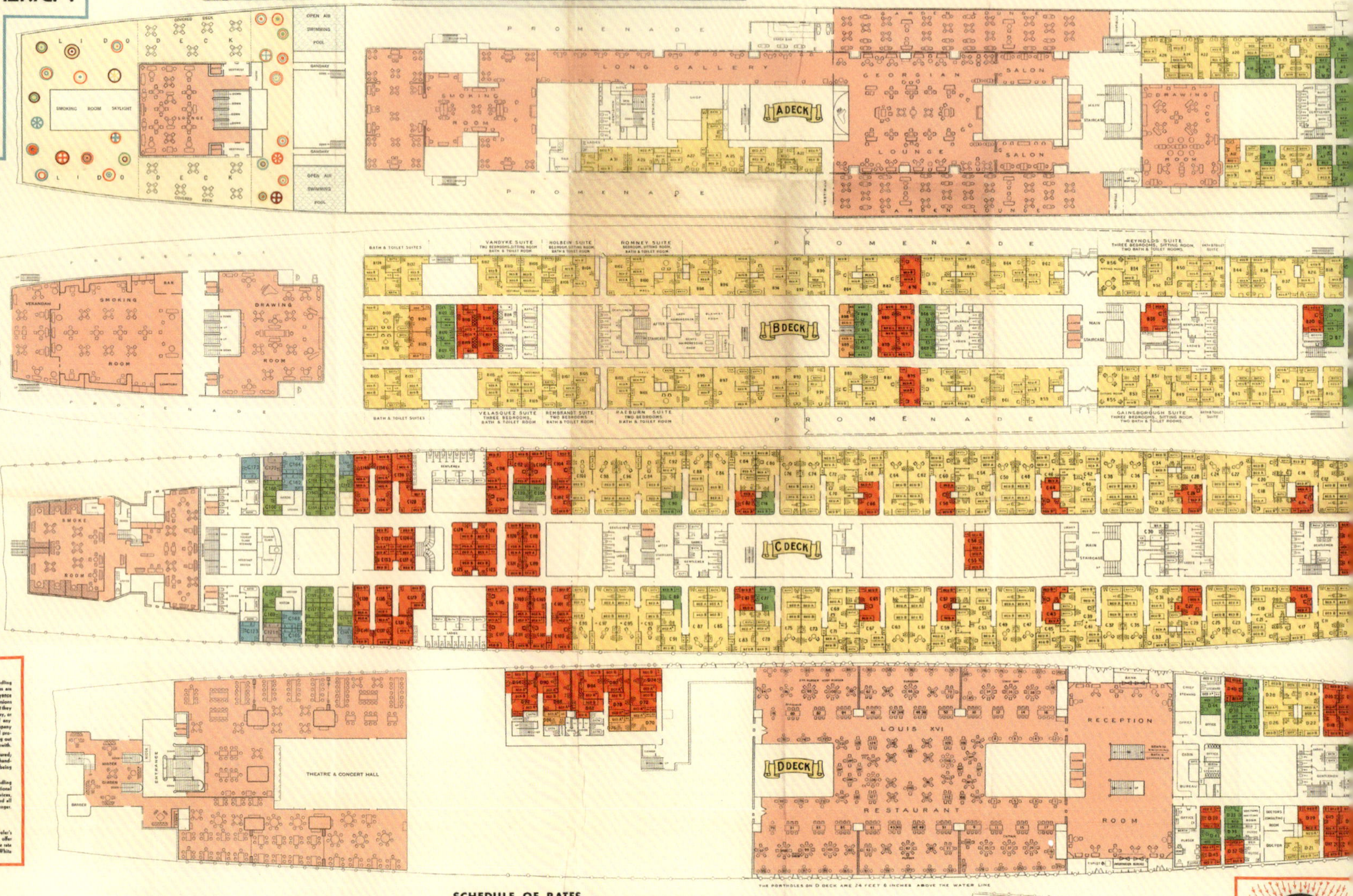

DIAGRAM TO SHOW LOCATION OF DECKS OF S. S. AQUITANIA

KEY FOR COLORS
- PUBLIC ROOMS
- ROOMS & BATH & ROOMS EN SUITE
- DOUBLE BED ROOMS
- ROOMS WITH BED, AND UPPER BERTH
- ROOMS WITH UPPER AND LOWER BERTHS
- SINGLE ROOMS
- ROOMS WITH 3 BERTHS

KEY FOR SYMBOLS

H.B. – Hatboy
D.T. – Dressing Table
F.S. – Folding Seat
W.R./D – Wardrobe
S. – Settee
W.R. – Washbasin
W.R. – Washbasin
BED. – Red with Upper Berth

CRUISE INFORMATION

THE Cunard White Star Line and/or the Tourist Company handling shore excursions give notice that all tickets and coupons are issued by them, and all arrangements for transport or conveyance or for hotel services in connection with the shore excursions are made by them, as Agents, upon the express condition that they shall not be liable for any injury, damage, loss, accident, delay, or irregularity which may be occasioned either by reason of any defect in any vehicle, or through the acts or default of any company or person engaged in conveying the passenger, or any hotel proprietor or servant, or of any other person engaged in carrying out the arrangements of the tour(s), or otherwise in connection therewith.

Baggage is at "owner's risk" throughout the tour(s) unless insured; this also applies to all small packages, such as dressing cases, handbags, umbrellas, cameras, field-glasses, rugs, etc., these further being entirely under the care of the passenger.

The Cunard White Star Line and/or the Tourist Company handling shore excursions accept no responsibility for losses or additional expenses due to delays or changes in train, steamer, or other services, sickness, weather, strikes, war, quarantine, or other causes, and all such losses or expenses will have to be borne by the passenger.

BAGGAGE INSURANCE

The Cunard White Star Line's arrangements for insuring traveler's baggage against breakage, theft, loss, or fire, on land or sea, offer another valuable service to travelers well worth the moderate sum charged. Full particulars from your local agent or any Cunard White Star office.

Deck labels: A DECK · B DECK · C DECK · D DECK · E DECK

ITINERARY

Port	Arrive	Leave	Time in Port
NEW YORK		noon Wed. Feb. 17	
NASSAU	a.m. Sat. Feb. 19	2 a.m. Sun. Feb. 20	a day and evening
PANAMA	a.m. Wed. Feb. 23	p.m. Wed. Feb. 23	½ day and a night
LA GUAIRA	a.m. Fri. Feb. 25	6 p.m. Fri. Feb. 25	a day
TRINIDAD	a.m. Sat. Feb. 26	noon Sun. Feb. 27	a day and night
BAHIA	a.m. Fri. Mar. 4	p.m. Fri. Mar. 4	a day
RIO DE JANEIRO	a.m. Sun. Mar. 6	p.m. Thu. Mar. 10	4 days
BARBADOS	a.m. Wed. Mar. 16	p.m. Wed. Mar. 16	a day and a night
BERMUDA	a.m. Sun. Mar. 20	p.m. Sun. Mar. 20	a day
NEW YORK	a.m. Tues. Mar. 22		

Total cruise distance... 11,461 miles

SCHEDULE OF RATES

BOAT DECK	For One Alone	For Two Each
OUTSIDE ROOM with private bath		
O—bed, pullman berth	$1400	
Without private bath		
N, bed and pullman berth	785	
C, E, F, H, K, M, bed	700	
INSIDE ROOMS without private bath		
D, G, J, L, bed	550	

A DECK		
OUTSIDE ROOMS with private bath		
A—98, 25, 27, two beds	$1900	
A—9, 12, 15, 18, 19, 21, 22, 23, 24, 89, 99, 21, two beds, pullman berth	1150	
Without private bath		
A—1, 3, 5, 6, 8, bed	750	
INSIDE ROOMS without private bath	600	
A—17, 18, bed and pullman berth	575	
A—7, 10, 11, 14, bed		

B DECK		
VAN DYKE AND VELASQUEZ SUITES		
B—108, 110, 1109, Two bedrooms (four beds), sitting room	$1800	
B—108, 111, 1113, bath and toilet		
ROMNEY AND RAEBURN SUITES		
B—100, 1009, Bedroom (two beds), sitting room, bath and toilet	$2000	
B—102, 1029, toilet		
PARLOR SUITES		
B—50, 52	$2150	
B—48, 51		
B—53, 55	$2150	
B—54, 56		
B—108, 110		
B—109, 111		

B DECK (Continued)	For One Alone	For Two Each
OUTSIDE ROOMS with private bath		
B—47, 48, 49, 50, 58, 61, 62, 63, 64, 65, 66, 70, 81, 82, 83, 84, 92, 93, 94, 95, 96, 97, 98, 99, 100, 101, 106, 107, 108, 109, 112, 133, 134, 135, two or three beds	$1450	
B—76, 31, 32, 37, 38, 43, 44, two beds, pullman berth	1400	
B—53, 54, 130, 131, two beds	1350	
B—90, 91, bed	$1800	
Without private bath		
B—55, 58, 53, 56, 75, 76, 61, 82, 83, 84, 92, 93, 100, 103, 104, 105, 110, 111, 113, 115—two or three beds	900	
B—95, 98, two beds and pullman berth	900	
B—90, 91, bed	800	
B—1, 2, 3, 4, 5, 6, 8, bed		
INSIDE ROOMS without private bath		
B—30, 38, 116, 117, 118, 119, two beds and folding upper berth	575	
B—73, 74, 79, 80, two beds and upper berth	650	
B—104, 135, bed and upper berth	575	
B—7, 10, 180, 131, 132, bed	550	
B—67, 68, 69, 85, 86, 87, 88, 89, bed		

C DECK		
OUTSIDE ROOMS with private bath		
C—35, 36, 37, 38, 47, 48, 49, 50, 61, 62, 63, 64, 73, 74, 75, 85, 85, 86, 87, 88, 103, 104, 95, 98, 97, 98, 99, 100, two or three beds	$1850	
C—41, 42, 45, 46, 53, 54, 59, 60, 67, 68, 71, 72, two beds	$1900	
C—9, 10, 11, 12, 20, 23, 24, 25, two or three beds	1800	
C—79, 80, 83, 84, 91, 92, two beds, pullman berth	1050	
OUTSIDE ROOMS without private bath		
C—1, 2, 103, 104, 107, 108, 111, 112, 116, 117, 130, 137, 135, 137, 146, 147, two beds and pullman berth	800	

C DECK (Continued)	For One Alone	For Two Each
OUTSIDE ROOMS without private bath		
C—170, 171, two beds	$750	$575
C—3, 4, bed	735	
C—5, 6, bed	550	
C—144, 145, 164, 165, 172, 173, two berths	525	
C—158, 153, 160, 161, single berth		
Without private bath		
C—18, 19, 21, 30, 39, 40, 51, 52, 69, 70, two beds, pullman berth	900	775
C—7, 8, 14, 15, 26, 27, 43, 44, 57, 58, 65, 66, 87, 88, 101, 108, 105, 108, 114, 115, 125, 138, 139, 120, 133, 134, 135, 138, 139, two beds and pullman berth	900	
C—55, 56, 110, 119, 180, 181, 190, 193, 104, 105, two beds	575	
C—77, 78, 89, 90, 108, 110, bed	500	
C—102, 151, two berths		
C—143, 145, 146, 147, 148, 149, 150, 151, 154, 158, 156, 157, 158, 159, 160, 167, 168, 109, single berth	450	

D DECK		
OUTSIDE ROOMS with private bath		
D—21, 24, 38, two beds, pullman berth	1000	
OUTSIDE ROOMS without private bath		
D—8, 11, 16, 17, 20, 24, 28, 37, 40, 74, 80, 84, 90, 94, two beds	1000	
D—72, 78, 80, 88, 98, two beds, pullman berth	610	585
D—54, bed	710	
INSIDE ROOMS without private bath		
D—20, 88, two beds, pullman berth		650

D DECK (Continued)	For One Alone	For Two Each
INSIDE ROOMS without private bath		
D—5, 19, 14, 15, 18, 19, 20, 30, 39, 40, two beds		$415
D—1, 3, 4, 8, 30, 32, 33, 35, 38, 38, 41, 44, bed	$460	
D—70, 75, 80, bed, pullman berth	460	

Minimum Rate $415.00
Servant's Rate .... Minimum Rate in servants' accommodation

Extensions subject to change.
Rates do not include shore excursions.
Children under two years of age are not charged.
The Company reserves the right to refuse to sell rooms listed with bath without the bath or for less than capacity.
Children under ten years of age are charged half fare provided there are at least two adults in the room.

No Passports Required by U. S. or Canadian Citizens

All aliens whether temporarily or permanently domiciled in the United States are required to secure exit permits before embarking on voyage. Aliens in the U. S. on a temporary visit require a passport with an re-entry permit to insure re-entry.

TAXES, ETC.

The undermentioned taxes are additional to the cruise fare and will be collected at the time of issuance of the ticket.

PAYMENTS.—At time of booking—25 percent of cruise rate; balance (final payment)—January 5, 1938.

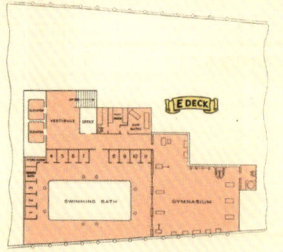

E DECK — SWIMMING BATH · GYMNASIUM

NOTE: FOLDING GUIDES AT TOP, BOTTOM AND SIDES

FRESH SEA AIR DRAWN DOWN THROUGH VENTILATOR

TO YOUR INSIDE STATEROOM

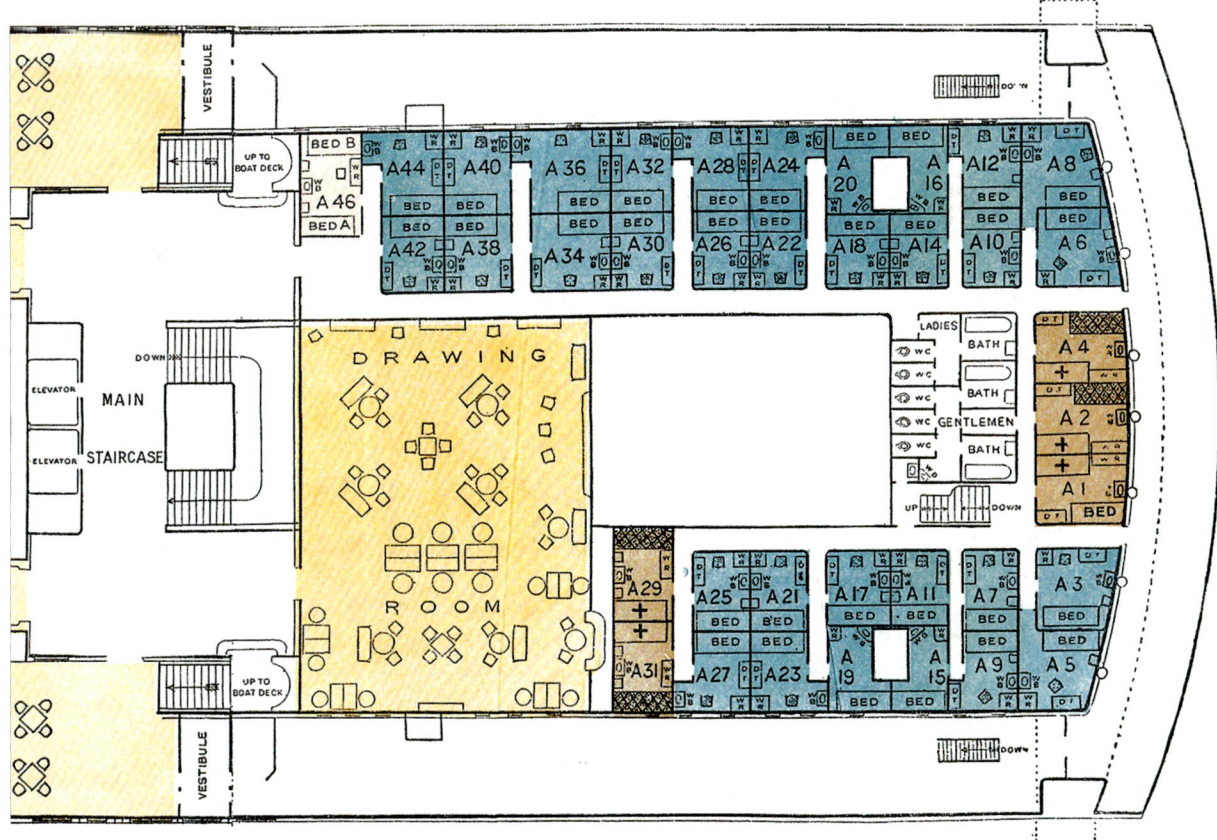

Opposite: This very rare colour-coded accommodation plan was issued in 1938. It is unusual because it shows both the first-class accommodation ('cabin class' from 1936) and the original second-class areas ('tourist class' after 1932–33). During the cruise, passengers had a free run of the ship. Not only does it show the detailed furniture layout, but it is interesting to compare the *Aquitania* of 1938 wih her 1914 arrangement (see pages 14–15). The changes are far too numerous to list here, but they include the expansion of the first-class suites on B-deck; the improved C-deck staterooms; the public rooms aft on C- and D-decks (which were originally added for tourist-third-class passengers in 1929); the removal of the first-class grill room on D-deck; and the partial conversion of the original second-class dining saloon to a cinema and a theatre. (Author's collection)

Right: The first-class staterooms forward on A- and B-decks, as depicted on a 1920 accommodation plan. Eighteen years later, many of these staterooms had been enlarged and private bathroom facilities added. A different colour-coding scheme was used from the 1938 plan opposite. (Author's collection)

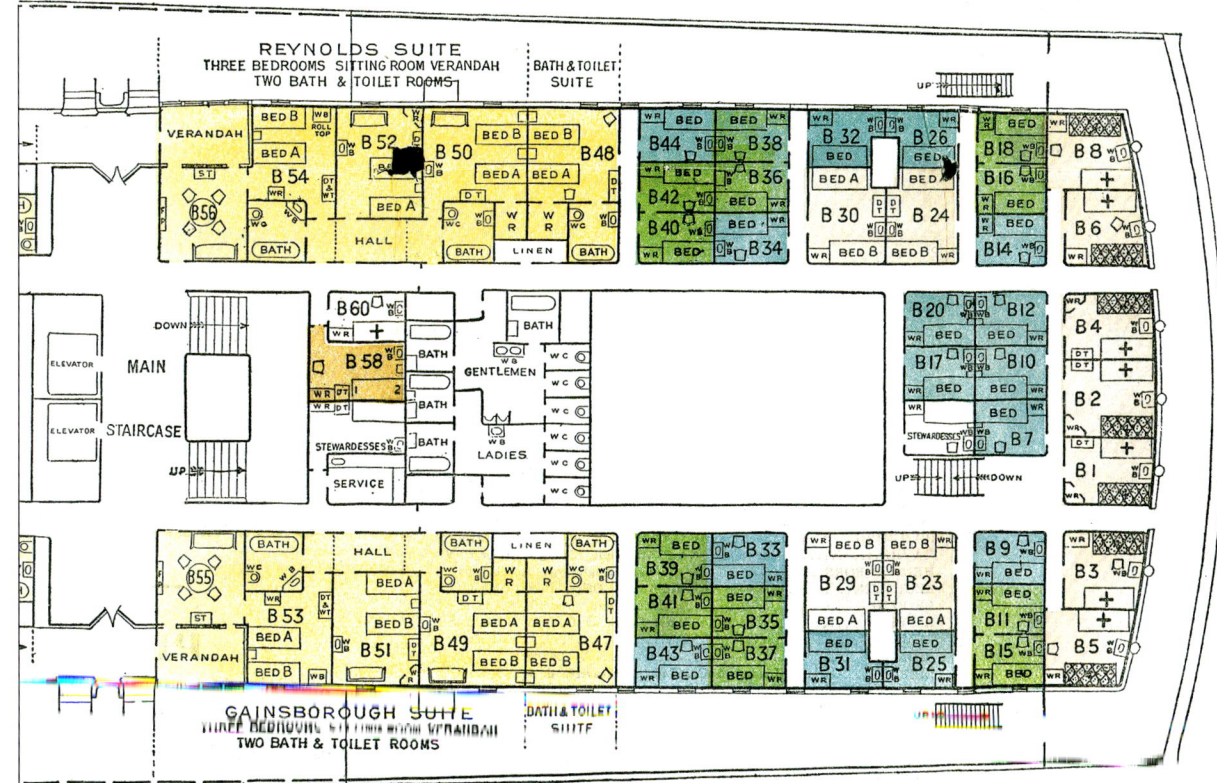

3 January 1934 for the voyage to New York, although she grounded briefly on her next Southampton departure twenty-one days later. On the last day of January she began her 225th round trip voyage, only completing the westbound leg because two Mediterranean cruises were scheduled. Yet she left New York on 7 March 1934 for her 227th eastbound departure, plying the Southampton to New York express route for the rest of the year. A planned 18 December Christmas cruise was cancelled, but there would be a number of cruises scheduled for 1935.

After leaving Southampton on 23 January 1935, *Aquitania* crossed to New York, departing on the last day of the month for a cruise to the Mediterranean. Almost 800 passengers were booked, including 368 in first class, 116 in tourist and 305 in third; enough to create a gross profit of £13,166 but not avoid a net loss of £5,674. By 9 March 1935, she was departing for another Mediterranean cruise, although this time her passenger list was shorter. There was some trouble as *Aquitania* was caught by a 50mph gale when she returned to Southampton in mid-April, grounding in Southampton Water. Many passengers were landed by tender, telling reporters that they had been unaware of the grounding until 'they felt the vessel tremble when her engines were put full speed astern.' Water and oil were removed, yet the efforts of nine straining tugs did not seem to help free the liner. She was stuck for twenty-four hours before being freed the following afternoon, crowds ashore cheering when 'a glorious rainbow, like some lucky emblem, was spanning the ship!' Fortunately, the hull appeared undamaged.

There were signs of improvement on the passenger front when *Aquitania* carried 1,013 passengers on her 26 June 1935 eastbound crossing, and had three four-figure passenger lists on her westbound departures between 14 August 1935–18 September 1935. This was better than a year earlier, and to make matters even better Cunard expected *Aquitania* to record a gross profit for 1935. Among the famous passengers *Aquitania* carried was J.B. Priestley, westbound for New York. He commented on the voyage in his autobiography:

She was the *Aquitania*, one of the pleasantest of the big liners, a comfortable, friendly, family party sort of boat. Nothing was wrong with what Americans call 'the set up.' Yet everything was wrong. I felt depressed, perhaps by the state of the world, perhaps by the state of my liver, when we left Southampton; and all the cocktails and caviare, deck tennis and table tennis, bridge and poker, talking pictures and talking passengers, provided by the Cunard White Star Company could not prevent my sinking into a deeper despondency. The sea may have had something to do with it. Lifts and glass-enclosed decks and garden lounges and steel shopping streets – and there is something almost heroic in the spectacular urban idiocies of these ships – cannot make you forget the presence of this huge element, at once so menacing and so melancholy.[3]

Aquitania began to experience the sort of problems common to older ships as she approached and surpassed the age of twenty. These were evident initially in the 1920s and were largely routine maintenance issues, yet localised signs of fatigue increased from the early 1930s. In 1936, her general structural condition was satisfactory, given her service history, and on 5 July 1938 a Board of Trade surveyor recorded that *Aquitania*'s hull plating 'generally is in good condition and the scantlings are well maintained.' Yet, when she arrived at Southampton on 20 September 1938, a strake of heavy hull plating was 'fractured right across through a line of rivets' amidships on B-deck.[4] Fortunately, the riveting remained sound, but the fracture was 'a definite through fracture' rather than a hairline crack. Creaking noises had been noticed months earlier. It was close to the region where cracked girders on B-deck had been repaired in 1931, although on the whole *Aquitania* remained in good condition as the decade drew to a close.

Mauretania, *Olympic* and *Majestic* had all made their final voyages by early 1936, leaving *Aquitania* and *Berengaria* in service prior to the *Queen Mary*'s debut that summer. Unfortunately, they were both much slower than the new liner. Early in 1934, Cunard had modified *Aquitania*'s condensers in an effort to increase her speed, yet the additional propeller slip prevented the ship from averaging the intended 24 knots. The problem was only remedied when new propellers were fitted in 1936 and the area of the blades increased from 103 to 125sq.ft. Cunard decided to use *Aquitania* as the primary running mate on the express service with the *Queen Mary*, as *Aquitania*'s operating costs were lower than *Berengaria* or *Majestic*. The surprise retirement of *Majestic* left *Berengaria* as the only suitable third vessel available.

In September 1936, Cunard had reason to be pleased. Even after the new *Queen Mary*'s debut, *Aquitania* and *Berengaria*'s average passenger carryings had risen. Cunard decided that *Aquitania*'s first-class grill room would be converted into passenger accommodation to meet the anticipated increase in passenger traffic in 1937. Another change was that, from 1936, *Aquitania*'s first-class passenger accommodation was termed 'cabin class' by the North Atlantic Conference.[5] Higher passenger lists materialised as expected; between 1934 and 1937 the number of round trips that *Aquitania* made annually increased from thirteen-and-a-half to eighteen, and passenger numbers rose from 13,317 to 26,389. In 1937, she averaged 733 passengers per crossing, very respectable in the circumstances.

Aquitania's busy year in 1937 did not get off to the best of starts, since she arrived in New York one-and-a-half days behind schedule, on 28 January 1937. Many of the more than 500 passengers described the crossing 'as the worst they had ever experienced', according to a *New York Times* reporter. Eleven large windows had been smashed by a 'giant wave' while woodwork had been splintered for up to 35ft. At the height of the storm, between the Saturday and

Sunday, the ship's noon-to-noon run came in at only 188 miles. Captain Irving said that the storm 'was as bad as any' that he had ever experienced.

In August 1937, the *New York Times* reported 'that she's a stout ship still, despite her three-and-twenty years, she proved handsomely earlier this week [sic] when she … broke many of the records of her youth and made one of the fastest western ocean crossings in history.' *Aquitania*'s eastbound crossing of 30 June 1937 was completed in just five days, nine hours and forty-two minutes, at an average speed of 24.7 knots, and the following crossings had also been impressive. The reporter continued:

> To the many who have trudged the long 'laps to a mile' around the *Aquitania*'s promenade, who have slept in her comfortable cabins and have felt the 'crash on her bows, dear lass, and the drum of the racing screw', it is clear that the old Cunarder is a spirited lady, good still for many more years of dignified but delightful service that has made her famous.

By the following year *Aquitania*'s schedule included thirteen-and-a-half round trips to New York and a number of cruises, as she retained a loyal following. Her gross tonnage was calculated at 44,786 gross tons in the late 1930s, whereas it had once stood at over 46,000. In May 1938, *Aquitania* crossed to New York at 24.4 knots, and her eastbound return at the start of June 1938 was even better when she increased her average speed to 24.8 knots. It might have been expected that *Aquitania* would do no better, but between 10 May and 23 May 1939 she completed two impressive crossings. Westbound, she sped to New York at an average of 23.9 knots, covering 3,194 miles in five days, thirteen hours and thirty-three minutes; while on the return she covered 3,239 miles in five days, nine hours and thirty-six minutes at an average speed of 24.99 knots.[6] The best day's run of 594 miles related to an average speed of 25.83[7] knots! *Aquitania* had averaged 22 knots in 1931, her average speed rising every year to 22.5 knots in 1934; she averaged 23.2 knots in 1937 and then a mighty 23.6 knots throughout 1938. *Aquitania* was still improving with age.

Cunard's fleet was changing dramatically by the late thirties. After a series of increasingly serious fires, *Berengaria* had been withdrawn from service in March 1938, when necessary re-wiring was considered uneconomic. That month the *New York Times* speculated that *Aquitania* might be withdrawn in two years' time when the *Queen Elizabeth* arrived.

In spite of the expectation that *Aquitania*'s days were numbered, the announcement of her retirement never came. However, there was some drama at the time of the Munich crisis. Newspaper reports late in September 1938 quoted Cunard White Star's announcement that *Aquitania* had been temporarily withdrawn from service, despite being scheduled to sail on 5 October 1938 with 'a large list of passengers'. (Her previous westbound voyage enjoyed a bumper list of 1,465.) It was understood that she would be 'used as a troop transport in the event of international conflict' and she reportedly arrived 'in Port Said laden with troops' while she was off the Atlantic.[8] *Aquitania* then spent much of her time cruising before returning to the express service with her 3 December 1938 westbound departure.

Captain Gibbons described a typical storm in January 1939 which made *Aquitania* eight hours late and cut her average speed to below 21 knots. In February 1939, the year ahead looked set to be a good one. Cunard White Star's general passenger manager, H. Borer, told reporters that bookings for Cunard's express ships has risen by 22 per cent compared to the same time a year earlier: 'Every express sailing of the line has shown marked improvement over comparable sailings in 1938', he enthused. *Aquitania*'s first voyage had improved her cabin-class bookings by 100 per cent over the same one the previous year, while her first three voyages of 1939 showed passenger lists around 18 per cent higher. As the summer of 1939 passed the express service was working flat out, and when the war began it became clear that the twenty-five-year old *Aquitania* would be needed for years to come. *Aquitania* was set on a course that would stretch her living days beyond the following decade.

NOTES

1 Braynard Volume 5, page 94.

2 McCart's *Atlantic Liners*, page 105.

3 Priestley, J.B. *Midnight on the Desert*. Heinemann; 1937, page 15. Reproduced from *Midnight on the Desert* by J.B. Priestley (Copyright: Estate of J.B. Priestley 1937) by permission of PFD (www.pfd.co.uk) on behalf of the Estate of J.B. Priestley.

4 A 'strake' is defined as a row of longitudinal (fore and aft) hull plating along the liner's side.

5 Sometimes referred to as the 'Transatlantic Passenger Conference' or, more fully, the 'North Atlantic Passenger Conference' (NAPC).

6 Maritime Archives & Library, Merseyside Maritime Museum. Cunard collection, reference B/CUN/4/4/5. 1907–33 [sic].

7 Even detailed mechanical records survive. The average propellor 'revolutions per minute' were 162.5 over the crossing, while the best day's run was accomplished at 164.9 as the engines developed 58,545 shaft horsepower (or SHP). *Aquitania*'s oil consumption averaged 723.3 tons every twenty-four hours, working out to 1.162 pounds of fuel per shaft horsepower developed per hour. Surprisingly, *Aquitania* slowed down for two hours and twenty-two minutes to suit her scheduled arrival time, which reduced her average speed.

8 Hutchings, page 3.

Above left: *Aquitania*'s first-class main entrance was light and elegant, reminiscent of *Lusitania*'s interior décor. (*Railway & Travel Monthly*, 1914/J. & C. McCutcheon collection)

Above right: The drawing room for first class was 'a reproduction from the best period' of the Adam brothers, 1780, while the bookcases were made of Cuba mahogany. (*Railway & Travel Monthly*, 1914/J. & C. McCutcheon collection)

Centre left: *Aquitania*'s first-class lounge was 'reminiscent of the work of Sir Christopher Wren'. (*The Shipbuilder*, 1914/author's collection)

Centre right: 'A salon or writing room.' (*Railway & Travel Monthly*, 1914/J. & C. McCutcheon collection)

Below left: An impressive view of the Long Gallery, which stretched 'for nearly 150ft – from the first class smoking room to the lounge – on the A-deck.' (*The Shipbuilder*, 1914/author's collection)

Below right: One of *Aquitania*'s garden lounges seems rather empty in this period postcard. (Author's collection)

Justly described as 'magnificent', *Aquitania*'s first-class restaurant had a floor area of 13,500 square feet, or nearly one-third of an acre. 'The decoration is in the Louis XVI style, the woodwork is in panelled mahogany, and painted grey, the whole being enriched with carved ornament, and a beautiful arrangement of pilasters and columns.' (*Railway & Travel Monthly*, 1914/J. & C. McCutcheon collection)

First class's smoke room was superb, considered 'one of the most magnificent rooms on the vessel.' Solid oak panelling was evident, while a nautical flavour was obtained by the floor which was 'composed of oak deck boards of random widths, as used in old men-of-war.' The room was no less than 76ft long and 52ft wide at its extremities. (*Railway & Travel Monthly*, 1914/J. & C. McCutcheon collection)

Right: Although the décor was simpler than its first-class counterpart, the second-class dining saloon on board *Aquitania* was stylish and a marked improvement upon previous liners. While *Lusitania*'s swivel chairs were fixed to the deck – even in her first-class saloon – aboard *Aquitania* the chairs could be moved more freely, thus improving passenger comfort. (*Railway & Travel Monthly*, 1914/J. & C. McCutcheon collection)

Above left: The second-class drawing room was typical of the improvements *Aquitania* offered. Decorated in Adam style, the room was furnished with 'tasteful antique mahogany Hepplewhite furniture'. (*Railway & Travel Monthly*, 1914/J. & C. McCutcheon collection)

Left: *Aquitania*'s swimming bath. The walls were panelled with teak, while the floor covering was cork, staining its natural colour with a slightly oiled surface. (*Railway & Travel Monthly*, 1914/J. & C. McCutcheon collection)

Aquitania left Southampton on 23 August 1939 for New York via Cherbourg, her passengers including Lord Lothian, who was the new British Ambassador to the United States. Six days later she arrived in New York, but although she was scheduled to sail for Southampton the following day the American authorities decided to search the ship for any war materials. The German liner *Bremen* was delayed for two days, while the French Line's *Normandie* was also searched. In the event she left New York a few hours late, at 6.30 p.m. on 30 August 1939. By the time she arrived back in Southampton on 5 September 1939, with the ex-Ambassador to the United States, Sir Ronald Lindsay, Britain had been at war with Germany for two days. She completed another round trip to New York before the end of September, before being laid up at Cowes. On 10 October 1939, the Admiralty wrote to Cunard and instructed them not to sail the *Queen Mary*, the new *Mauretania* or *Aquitania*.

It became clear that she would be needed for government service, and sure enough she was requisitioned on 18 November 1939 by the Ministry of Shipping 'for service as a transport under charter party T.97.' Accommodation was provided for 262 officers, 258 warrant officers, and 2,330 other ranks, for a total of 2,850 troops (later increased by 34); the crew numbered 534 (including 98 deck hands, 156 in the engine department and 280 caterers). The officers' accommodation was located on the boat, A- and B-decks, while the warrant officers enjoyed accommodation on B- and C-decks. Meanwhile, C-deck, D-deck, E-deck and F-deck's first-, tourist- and third-class areas served the troops, with the third-class lounge being fitted with hammocks for 124 people. Eating arrangements are recorded, as the first-class restaurant was utilised for officers (with warrant officers on the starboard side). The cinema became the sergeants' mess, while 1,050 troops ate in the tourist saloon and 1,262 in third class – both in two sittings.

On 29 November 1939, she departed on her 329th voyage, to Halifax. By 17 December 1939, she had returned to Greenock (Gourock) with the first contingent of Canadian troops, before continuing back to Southampton. Sadly, *Aquitania*'s service was marred that very morning. *Empress of Britain* and *Aquitania* were running parallel as part of a convoy. The aircraft carrier *Furious* was leading, while several escorts surrounded the liners. Around 4.20 a.m., in position 55°30′ North 06°54′ West, conditions were 'overcast and very dark', and a darkened ship (later identified as *Samaria*) was observed by the escort *Eskimo* on *Eskimo*'s starboard bow. *Eskimo*'s commander and the officer of the watch felt that *Samaria* would pass between *Eskimo*'s starboard side and *Furious*' port side without any problem. Things did not look that way on board *Furious*, as Captain Clarke remembered:

> The Officer of the Watch, Lieutenant Commander R.C.V. Thomson, RN (retd), was examining the lights of a vessel which he had just sighted on the port bow when the leading signalman of the Watch reported a darkened ship right ahead. The ship appeared to be too big to be a destroyer on the screen and the Officer of the Watch decided that she was approaching so rapidly that he had to turn *Furious* independently of the convoy. He ordered 'Starboard 15 [degrees]', reported the ship down the voice pipe to me and then ordered 'Starboard 35 [degrees]'. Almost immediately he noticed, and at the same time heard a confirmatory report from the signal deck, that the ship was crossing from port to starboard. He ordered 'midships' and then 'Port 35 [degrees]' and then 'amidships' and blew two blasts on [the] siren. The ship then passed close down the starboard side of the *Furious* carrying away all three wireless transmission masts which were in the lowered position …

Having damaged *Furious*, *Samaria* collided with *Aquitania*'s port quarter at around 4.30 a.m. The collision 'was clearly audible, and visible due to sparks', according to *Eskimo*'s commander. *Eskimo* stopped and switched on her navigation lights,

Her superstructure painted grey, *Aquitania* arrives in New York on 16 September 1939. (Author's collection)

as there was a concern the *Samaria* would sink. *Empress of Britain* had seen the *Samaria*-*Aquitania* collision and altered course to port. As a result of the course change, *Eskimo* had to go 'full ahead' to avoid her. Fortunately, it turned out that *Samaria* was 'in no danger of sinking', and damage to the *Aquitania* was relatively minor. These events helped highlight the problems with navigating convoys, as in this case all ships had only been displaying their stern lights, while travelling at 17 knots. Another key issue was communication. On 29 December 1939, Admiral Forbes of HMS *Warspite* commented that, 'the basic cause of SS *Samaria* and the convoy meeting at all was the fact that the Naval Control Officer, Liverpool, did not know of the convoy's existence'.

Aquitania sailed on government service from Southampton on 16 January 1940, to Halifax and Gourock, returning on 14 February 1940. Six days later Cunard recorded that she had been dry-docked, and would be discharged from the government's service after the operation was completed. Yet *Aquitania* was requisitioned for government service before another month had passed, and on 9 March 1940 she sailed from Southampton for Freetown, Cape Town, then to Fremantle, Sydney and Wellington, New Zealand.

For her 332nd voyage, *Aquitania* left Wellington on 2 May 1940 for Fremantle, Cape Town, Simonstown, Freetown, Greenock and Liverpool, where she arrived on 22 June 1940, just as France collapsed. *Aquitania*'s troop capacity varied as accommodation changed and improved over her years of war service.

Above right: Aquitania ploughing through the sea on 7 March 1944. She would arrive in New York two days later. (Royal Canadian Airforce photo from the Maritime Museum of the Atlantic)

Centre right: Steaming across calm seas, a rust-scarred *Aquitania*, shown around 1944. Note that a number of lifeboats have been swung out. The heavy corrosion seen beneath the curved shelter deck bulwark, where the superstructure front ends before the bow, may have been aggravated by the 30in crack in this plating that appeared a decade earlier (see page 63). (From the collection of the Maritime Museum of the Atlantic)

Below right: On 2 March 1946, *Aquitania* is shown at Halifax with a number of war brides. She appears to have a slight list to port, presumably as the crowds gather on that side of the ship. (Haywood photo from the collection of the Maritime Museum of the Atlantic)

It is 9 June 1946 and *Aquitania* is shown at Halifax, her decks crowded, with the North Nova Scotia Highlanders onboard. (From the collection of the Maritime Museum of the Atlantic)

A fantastic view from the port side. (From the collection of the Maritime Museum of the Atlantic)

She carried 172 officers, 193 warrant officers and sergeants, and 2,708 other ranks, for a total of 3,073 troops; her berthing capacity had been increased during her last stop at Sydney to 3,284 by providing 208 additional berths on A, B and C-decks, and constructing 96 berths in each of the two garden lounges. At Wellington, 64 berths in each of the garden lounges had been removed and 86 new berths provided in the lounge aft on A-deck. When all the work was completed, after a number of other changes, *Aquitania*'s capacity fell back to 3,238. The hammocks for 124 troops in the third-class lounge were only used for part of the voyage, yet the ship was blessed with good weather.

During the darkest years of the war, for two years from the summer of 1940, *Aquitania*'s war service took her all over the globe. Seven days after arriving at Liverpool, she left for Freetown, Cape Town, Simonstown and Colombo; she was to travel as far afield as Bombay, Singapore

(where she was dry-docked early in 1941), Suez, Trincomalee, Port Tewfik, Port Moresby, Ratui Bay, Honolulu, San Pedro, Panama, New York, Clyde, Aden, Diego Suarez, Boston and Rio de Janeiro. Three years into the war, she had been in service for twenty-eight years: one year more than *Mauretania*, and twenty years longer than the ill-fated *Lusitania*, her original two running mates.

Aquitania began a remarkable feat when she left New York on 21 September 1942 for Rio de Janeiro, with her oil-carrying capacity expanded to enable her to make the voyage. All in all, it took twelve days at an average speed of 21 knots, and two days' worth of oil was left over. Yet on the departure from Rio de Janeiro she was so heavily loaded that she was drawing 38ft 9in of water forward, and 37ft 9in of water aft. Carrying 7,000 troops, their baggage, and necessary army and ship's stores for twenty-five days, *Aquitania* was overloaded by about 3,500 tons – undoubtedly a significant strain on her hull. She arrived in Cape Town on 13 October 1942, leaving for Suez via Aden. She left Suez on 3 November 1942, stopping at Aden (where she took on oil) on the way to Wellington, New Zealand, where she arrived on 27 November 1942 (having called at Fremantle for provisions). By the time she arrived, *Aquitania* had travelled around 27,000 miles without steam having been off the main engines.

There was a short reprieve before she was loaded with a full complement of New Zealand troops. *Aquitania* left Wellington on 12 December 1942 for Suez (Port Tewfik) via Fremantle, yet a planned call at Aden for fuel had to be abandoned at the authorities' request; by the end of the fourteen-day, thirteen-hour voyage there was less than two days' worth of oil left. The next port of call was Massawa, where she anchored for twelve days, but *Aquitania* returned to Suez on 23 January 1943 to embark a full complement of Australian troops and stores, 'proceeding again to Massawa where she stayed for three days and left in convoy for Fremantle and Sydney.' At His Majesty's Naval Base East Indies, *Aquitania* again took on oil, and stores and water were loaded from the *Queen Mary*. After an uneventful voyage *Aquitania* returned to Sydney in late February 1943. Weeks went by before she left for Cape Town, where she docked on 10 April 1943 and embarked prisoners of war and troops, being re-routed to Rio de Janeiro and New York, where she arrived on 4 May 1943. Around this time, it appears that *Aquitania*'s armament was upgraded from the 4.7in guns originally installed at New York to two 6in guns. The guns' presence created a good impression of confidence in the ship, along with the British and United States gunnery personnel who were on board and who worked together extremely well.

As 1943 wore on, and after nearly four years of strenuous wartime service, it became increasingly clear that the fortunes of war had moved against the Axis

Right: Aquitania docked at New York at the end of the Second World War. Taken by John Blake, it is one of many colour photographs that he took of *Aquitania* in the 1940s. (John Blake photo, Richard I. Weiss collection)

Below: Although her bow is not in the picture, *Aquitania*'s profile is impressive, as are her gleaming black funnel tops. (John Blake photo, Richard I. Weiss collection)

powers. Yet there was plenty of work left to do, and *Aquitania* was to join the growing number of ships carrying American service personnel to Europe for the upcoming invasion of the German-occupied continent. *Aquitania* returned to the Clyde, serving the North Atlantic ferry between Clyde and New York, from her 31 May 1943 Clyde departure until 29 June 1944. There was a small change to her regular schedule from 3 July 1944, when she began a series of four voyages between Clyde and Halifax, before returning to the Clyde-New York service for eight voyages until 16 May 1945. In December 1944, *Aquitania* was reportedly fitted with new propellers 'designed to increase her speed by one knot'.[1]

Life on board during the Second World War was similar to that during the earlier conflict. Penny Martin recalled her voyage on the *Aquitania* in the summer of 1942, as a Wren.[2] At Greenock she embarked on a tender before being shipped out to the four-funnelled Cunarder, and going aboard to a single cabin which held six people in two three-tier bunks. The ship sailed at 6.30 p.m. on 31 May 1942, sailing as part of a convoy which included HMS *Nelson*, and she wrote, 'I shall never forget the beauty of that trip down the River and into the Firth of Clyde. We came down between the Isle of Arran and the Scottish coast, and the view westward as the sun set was breathtaking.' It was the last she was to see of her native shores for more than two years.

'We were housed – twenty-four of us WRNS ratings – down one little side passageway off the main gangway, and at the end of our passage stood a marine sentry!' she wrote. Water was in short supply, with all baths using salt water. 'Our "messing" was pretty nice', she said, '– we fed "first sitting" in the main dining room along with the navy and military warrant officers and senior chiefs (the officers had the "second sitting"). But the food, although hardly what the Cunard [Line] would have provided in peacetime, was quite miraculously good to us – used only to wartime naval rations.' As one of the

Crewmen at t stern provide sense of scale this slide. (Joh Blake photo, Richard I. We collection)

In this fantasti image, *Aquitar* backs from the pier. The plum of white smok from the tug almost entirely obscures her f funnel. (John Blake photo, Richard I. We collection)

Aquitania was photographed at Southampt in 1948. This image was subsequently used as a postcard. (Ian Boyle collection, courtesy of Richard Weiss

Above and top: John Blake took a series of photos of *Aquitania*'s funnels at Halifax. These scarce slides show her under different lighting conditions and offer unusual vantage points. (John Blake photo, Richard I. Weiss collection)

Above right: Docked at Halifax, this view shows the detail of the riveting in *Aquitania*'s upperworks. The sheer of the decks is clearly visible. (John Blake photo, Richard I. Weiss collection)

Below right: Blake even photographed the ship's name at the stern. (John Blake photo, Richard I. Weiss collection)

Above left: In this shot taken from the railway, perhaps from a slow-moving train, *Aquitania* can be seen as well as Cunard's newer *Queen Elizabeth*. Seeing the two ships together demonstrates the advances in marine engineering during the years that separated them. (John Blake photo, Richard I. Weiss collection)

Above right: Queen Mary and *Aquitania* lie along the quay at Southampton's Western Docks near Berth 108, which a decade earlier had been the 'graveyard' of earlier liners, including *Mauretania* and *Olympic*. (John Blake photo, Richard I. Weiss collection)

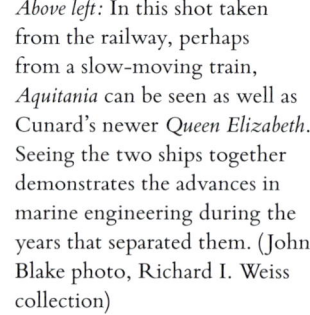

Right: Aquitania with *Queen Mary* in the distance. A lovely, playful funnel design fills the foreground. (John Blake photo, Richard I. Weiss collection)

Left, centre and bottom: Two fine shots of *Aquitania*, apparently taken from Southampton's Millbrook railway station. (John Blake photo, Richard I. Weiss collection)

Below: A wonderful view of *Aquitania* at sunset, against the quay of the 'New Docks' (or Western Docks) which were made from hundreds of acres of reclaimed land. The 'New Docks' was opened on 19 October 1932 by *Mauretania*. (John Blake photo, Richard I. Weiss collection)

only stenographers, she was 'nabbed' by an officer and spent two days sitting 'doing little' but pounding a typewriter and feeling 'put upon'.

She remembered that the convoy was slow (the convoy's speed being dictated by that of the slowest vessel) and in order to avoid U-boats they had sailed a long way to the west, with *Aquitania* leaving the convoy on 7 June 1942. The powers that be had decided *Aquitania* was safer alone, by virtue of her speed, although Penny Martin was mistaken when she said that she 'could still whack it up to thirty knots.' Six days later, the shortage of water (making the laundry impossible) meant that the Wrens were allowed to wear plain clothes, although it was not until 19 June 1942 that the ship approached the Cape of Good Hope, with the 'prospect of getting ashore in Cape Town.' Due to logistics, she did not get the chance to go ashore, and there were further problems as *Aquitania* drew too much water to enter Table Bay.

Three days later, *Aquitania* sailed up the east coast of Africa, and by lunchtime on 29 June 1942 she went on deck and saw the coastline of Madagascar, while at 4 p.m. they reached the harbour of Diego Suarez (now Autsiranana). Sandy hills and a few animals 'which may have been water buffalo' could be seen, but there was no sign of human life. *Aquitania* took on oil, before heading north – and experiencing a U-boat alert in the middle of the night a few days later. By 8 July 1942, they reached the Gulf of Suez,

Right: This wonderful composition looks forward from the aft starboard boat deck. Taken by John Blake on 8 January 1949, *Aquitania*'s raked funnels, lifeboats, deck fittings and ventilators bring to mind the classic old-fashioned steamship. (John Blake photo, Richard I. Weiss collection)

Below, right: An evocative and stunning view, with a beautiful lighting effect, captured late in the day during lively seas. (John Blake photo, Richard I. Weiss collection)

Below, centre: A fine view of the huge cowl ventilators that dominated *Aquitania*'s boat deck. A small group of passengers chat as they take the sea air. (John Blake photo, Richard I. Weiss collection)

Above left: After thirty-five years' service, *Aquitania* is along the quay at the 'New Docks' as she awaits her fate. Less than two years later, she would be a mere memory. (John Blake photo, Richard I. Weiss collection)

Below left: Even alongside newer ships, *Aquitania*'s profile and size are impressive. (John Blake photo, Richard I. Weiss collection)

disembarking to go on board the *Princess Kathleen*. *Aquitania* sailed a few days later, and Penny Martin remembered seeing the *Queen Elizabeth* arrive with around 10,000 troops onboard.

On Tuesday 12 October 1943, John William 'Jack' Clay was among a crowd of troops standing on the jetty at Gourock, surveying the scene on the Clyde, before being ferried out to the *Aquitania*.[3] 'In our part of the ship were units of the Canadian Forestry Corps who had spent two or three years in Scotland. There was [sic] American naval personnel too. We were without escort, depending on speed and alteration of course to throw off U-boats. Right aft two 6in guns were mounted', he remembered. In contrast to some soldiers' recollections from the ship during the First World War, Clay's diary continued:

> Every morning, much to our disgust, everyone had to fall in at boat stations or, in naval terms, 'Abandon ship stations.' There we stood for well over an hour, wearing life-belts and this happened each day throughout the voyage. It was very boring for us but I suppose it was carried out for the benefit of the civilian passengers. I was detailed for a lifeboat crew. Feeding was on Army lines. The food was very poor indeed and as there were so many to be catered for, one was admitted by ticket to the dining room at a specified time. Although we were detailed for working parties there was very little work to do and we were more

fortunate that the maritime gunners who, taking passage like we were, had to keep watches.

Just under a week later, at 7.30 p.m. on Monday 18 October 1943, *Aquitania* reached Halifax in the midst of a downpour. Since some of the dockyard workers were on strike, it took a meeting with union officials to resolve the situation, and even then the troops had to do much of the work of raising their possessions and equipment from the ship's holds. It took the entire night. 'Anyone who has served in the navy will tell of the appalling waste of time which occurs in British dockyards in wartime,' Clay wrote.

Alister Satchell, a lieutenant in the Royal Australian Navy Volunteer Reserve, contributes an extensive account of his time as one of the two cipher officers. He recalls sailing for New York on 29 November 1943. At 9.30 a.m., north of Ireland, speed had been reduced to 8 knots due to a gale when a floating mine was detected and, thanks to evasive action *Aquitania* missed it by a mere fifty yards.[4] 'Had the ship been making her usual 21 knots, we may well have struck the mine', he states. Writing of numerous escapes from U-boats, he remembers a particularly bad January 1944 storm. As *Aquitania* began to descend from the crest of a wave, 'the propellers would break the surface, evidenced by the vibrations from the accelerating shafts', yet she withstood the torture:

John Blake captioned this photograph as '*Aquitania* Finale': *Aquitania* at Faslane, early 1950. (John Blake photo, Richard I. Weiss collection)

Docked at Southampton in early December 1949, *Aquitania* had completed her final crossing from Halifax and the decision on her future was about to be announced. This photograph dates from around that time. (John Blake photo, Richard I. Weiss collection)

An impressive view of *Aquitania*'s stern while docked at Southampton in October 1948. (J. & C. McCutcheon collection)

Aquitania at Southampton in the late 1940s, her bow paintwork clearly having seen better days. Yet her white superstructure and gleaming funnels appear, at a glance, as good as new. (Clyde George collection)

> … in spite of her many protests in the form of creaking, groaning, vibrating and thumping, the Old Lady, proclaimed to be unrivalled as a seaboat, showed she was more than a match for anything the Atlantic could contrive to test her. On the eighth day [of the voyage], speed was reduced on account of a growing fuel shortage, the one thing every wartime strategy aimed to avoid.[5]

Captain Ford was relieved that the storm damage was not more extensive. The 'weather-scarred and rust-stained' *Aquitania* would have to wait many weeks for repairs and a fresh coat of paint.[6]

From May 1945 to early October 1945, *Aquitania* was involved in repatriating American and Canadian servicemen, yet she was withdrawn from the American service to help return British and Dominion troops home. While

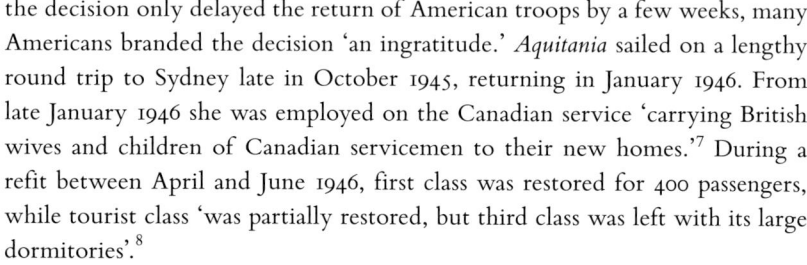

This is a particularly fine view of *Aquitania*'s bow and bridge front at the bottom left, photographed from the stem. (McBride photo from the collection of the Maritime Museum of the Atlantic)

The final farewell: *Aquitania* leaves Southampton for the last time. (J. & C. McCutcheon collection)

the decision only delayed the return of American troops by a few weeks, many Americans branded the decision 'an ingratitude.' *Aquitania* sailed on a lengthy round trip to Sydney late in October 1945, returning in January 1946. From late January 1946 she was employed on the Canadian service 'carrying British wives and children of Canadian servicemen to their new homes.'[7] During a refit between April and June 1946, first class was restored for 400 passengers, while tourist class 'was partially restored, but third class was left with its large dormitories'.[8]

In November 1946, an official at the Ministry of Transport considered *Aquitania*'s future in the event that she was released from their service in the first half of 1947. He reported that Cunard White Star's Mr Crail 'considered that there might well be paying use for her in her old trade fully reconverted and reconditioned for about four years. His information was that the hull and engines were quite sound and would be serviceable for at least that time.' The emigrant run to Australia was another option, requiring relatively minor work. In the event, there was enough need for the ship for the Canadian government to contract her for another year from April 1947.[9] The question was for how much longer employment could be found for the old liner.

NOTES

1 Satchell, pages 207–08.

2 Details of Mrs Penny Martin's voyage taken from IWM reference 02/36/1. She wrote her account in the 1980s and 1990s.

3 Details of writer John William Clay's voyage taken from IWM reference 01/2/1. His memories of his journey were mostly written in 1944, and finished in 1949.

4 Satchell, page 143.

5 Satchell, pages 159 and 161. He also notes (page 173) that in another storm in February 1944, *Queen Elizabeth*'s 'foredeck was crushed down several inches, opening up large cracks' and her below decks were buckling.

6 Satchell, page 161.

7 *Aquitania*, page 63.

8 McCart's *Atlantic Liners*, page 106.

9 *Aquitania*, page 64.

seven

A CAREER'S CLOSE

*A*quitania proved that she still had a great deal of usefulness left in her, for she was to serve once again on the Canadian service. On 25 May 1948, *Lloyd's List* reported that *Aquitania* was now painted in her Cunard White Star colours for the first time since 1939, and was 'dressed overall in celebration of her return to service in yet another stage of her noted and lengthy career.' Cunard White Star and the Canadian government had signed an agreement for the use of the old liner to carry emigrants to the dominions, initially for a year. An average of 1,400 shipyard workers had been employed, and had refitted the liner since her transport service was terminated at the end of March 1948:

> While full reconditioning has not been undertaken the passenger accommodation in both the first and tourist classes offers a reasonable standard of comfort. She is scheduled to make eleven round [trip] voyages between Southampton and Halifax by the end of the year, and the first five westbound trips are already fully booked. She will have priority berths for 1,100 British emigrants on each trip, in addition to about 650 first class passengers.
>
> The tourist accommodation for the emigrants consists of cabins with four, six and eight berths and dormitories with twenty as the maximum number. The first class passengers are berthed in two-, four-, and six-berth cabins. The public rooms for both classes offer ample space and comfort, and much of the furniture in the first class public rooms, which was stored during the war and has now been returned onboard, represents some of the finest reproduction classical furniture ever to be made for a ship. The most notable pieces are to be seen in the James II smoking room, which is built of English oak, and the Georgian lounge.

The Times said that the first-class smoking room looked as it had been done thirty-four years before. Tourist-class accommodation consisted of the combined third- and tourist-class areas from the ship's pre-war configuration, while the ship's crew would number around 790. The wartime sergeants' mess, apparently the pre-war cinema, had become a children's playroom equipped with the most up-to-date toys. Among other things, between January and May 1948 nearly £71,000 was spent in the ship's engine department, almost £39,000 in the marine department and £132,000 in the furnishing department.

Mr. C.E. Pierce, a deputy general manager of the Cunard White Star Ltd., said that very little had been done to restore the vessel to her 1939 standard, and the aims were to put the ship into service with the minimum of delay and to make her capable of carrying a large number of emigrants to Canada. The bulk of the Canadian brides, some 40,000, had travelled by the liner following the completion of the task of carrying thousands of Canadian servicemen across the Atlantic. Much of the accommodation which was used for the Canadian brides had been brought into use for the new traffic which the liner was being called upon to carry … The present sailing schedule provided for a sailing from Southampton every three weeks until the end of the year; after that, much would depend on circumstances and conditions as they appeared to be at the end of the year. On her eastbound passages, the ship would bring dollar-earning passengers to this country.

Those who had booked their passage through Cunard White Star numbered 27,873 passengers in 1948, a figure which rose to 31,220 for 1949. Her total carryings were significantly higher, and high demand led to the Canadian agreement being renewed in 1949 for the year. The Canadian government agreed to contribute £80,000 to the cost of the voyages. Yet, even if *Aquitania* was carrying more people than she had typically carried each year in the 1920s and 1930s, she was now thirty-five years old. Even the 'old granny' could not go on defying time forever. Had she been withdrawn from service by the end of 1940, her career would still have been long and successful – her final decade of hard work is astonishing.

By late October 1949, the Ministry of Transport were aware that Cunard White Star's 'preliminary view' as to the *Aquitania*'s future was that 'they would not be justified, in view of the ship's age, in incurring the expense of surveys and repairs that would be required in their ordinary North Atlantic service, either with her existing "austerity" accommodation or fully reconverted.' From the Ministry's point of view, it would be of 'considerable assistance' if the liner 'could be kept going even to the end of the next tourist season (say October, 1950).' It was not to be.

On 15 November 1949, she left Southampton for Halifax via Cherbourg. Five days later, Halifax's radio station, CHNS, did a broadcast featuring *Aquitania*, giving a potted history of her, and stating that she could carry 1,708 passengers and 715 crew. 'Surely the people of Halifax have almost a feeling of part ownership in this great ship', the narrator said, later referring to persistent rumours as to her impending retirement:

> All ships must have an end to their lives, and that will be true of this one. When the time does come, and many of us in Halifax hope it will be long delayed, there will be real feeling of sorrow in the hearts of many of our people. We have come to accept the big four-stacker as really a part of Halifax. We would all miss its periodic presence at the seawall on our waterfront. So have a good look at her when she arrives tomorrow evening for another of her welcome visits to Halifax.

Little did he know that it would be her final arrival. On 24 November 1949, *Aquitania* left for ever. She returned to Southampton, completing the eastbound crossing at an average of 18.24 knots. In the late 1940s, the six boilers in Boiler Room 2 (out of the twenty-one boilers in total) were unused, reducing her 'general speed' in service from the original 23 knots to 18.5 knots.

By 12 December 1949, Cunard White Star concluded that, 'In the circumstances it is not proposed to operate the vessel further in the company's service. The ship has been in commission since 30 May 1914.' After a 'preliminary inspection' on the first day of the month by Lloyd's and Ministry of Transport surveyors, it was found that a special survey was required – along with any necessary work – before *Aquitania* could continue

in service. Unfortunately, it was anticipated that the survey would be 'of an expensive character' and 'the work required would be in the nature of a major refit.' The company issued a statement two days later: 'After full consideration of all relevant circumstances it has been decided to withdraw the *Aquitania* from active service.'

It was received with sadness. Three days later *The Journal of Commerce* wrote, 'In fact, a decade ago it was regarded as significant that in the last sailing list issued by her owners before the war, the *Aquitania* did not appear after March 1940, hence it was generally assumed that as soon as the *Queen Elizabeth* entered service the *Aquitania* would be taken out of it.' The article speculated, 'That this [scrapping] may be delayed by finding employment for her as an hotel for tourists if possible.' The *Sunday Express* wrote on 18 December 1949 that *Aquitania* 'was the finest money spinner in the way of a liner yet built.' Meanwhile, *The Times* commented on her longevity on 15 December 1949, writing that after the 1936 arrival of the *Queen Mary*, 'At the end of each year the same old rumour came around – "the *Aquitania*'s finished" – but still those four funnels came serenely up Southampton water voyage after voyage.'

By 24 January 1950, the *Daily Graphic* was describing the quayside sheds near berth 108 as 'a vast furniture store'. *Aquitania*'s furnishings had been removed, and were sold over seven days from 13 February 1950. The auction catalogue ran to no less than eighty-five pages, as items ranging from dining room chairs to three dog kennels and all manner of fittings were listed. As for the liner herself, she had been bought for £125,000 by the British Iron and Steel Corporation. *Aquitania* left Southampton for the final time on Sunday 19 February 1950. Ahead lay a two-day voyage to the scrappers at Faslane, on the Clyde, where she would be dismantled from the superstructure down. It was a sad occasion for all concerned, yet shaped by the sad economic realities of post-war Britain.

Newspapers carried reports from Faslane on 12 October 1950 that the *Aquitania*'s bow section had caught fire. It was said that the fire 'roared through the hulk', with 'two fire companies and employees of the scrap-iron firm' fighting the fire for thirty minutes before bringing it under control. Although the bridge front remained, the superstructure amidships had all disappeared.

By the following summer, forty years had passed since her keel was laid, leading to remarkable changes ashore and on the Atlantic. Little remained of *Aquitania*'s hull, bar the staunch double-bottom structure. It marked the end of the line for one of the most successful and beloved ocean liners in history.

British Registry Details of RMS *Aquitania*

Official number of ship: 135,583

Length, between perpendiculars: 868ft 7in

Breadth: 97ft

Depth from top of deck at sides amidships to bottom of keel: 54ft 7½in

Particulars of displacement: 61,720 tons. Ditto per inch immersion at same depth: 146 tons

No. of sets of engines: four

No. of shafts: four

Description of engines: rotary direct acting

Name and address of makers: John Brown & Co., Clydebank

Rotary engines, no. of cylinders in each set: two

IHP: 56,000

Speed of ship: 23 knots

Particulars of tonnage: Gross tonnage 45,646.99. Net tonnage: 20,800.35 tons

Under tonnage deck: 17,996.64 tons

Dated: 26 May 1914

Number of shares: 64

In addition to her entry in the British registry, *Aquitania*'s statistics were recorded in other sources, such as a naval architects' data book, dated October 1919 (and updated in 1936):

General Particulars

Length, overall: 902ft

Breadth, moulded: 96ft 6in

Draught (full) keel: 34ft 10in

SHP: 56,000

Type of engines: four turbines

Freeboard, assigned: 19ft 6in

Length, between perpendiculars: 865ft

Depth, moulded: 54ft 6in

Displacement, S.W. (full) 49,430 tons

Steam pressure: 195psi

Revolutions per minute: 180rpm

Some of the differences between the registry details and other sources stem from a different method of measurement. For instance, the 'moulded breadth' of the ship will be narrower than the 'extreme breadth' of the ship, which includes the outer extremities of the hull plating and riveting.

Tonnage and Form Particulars

Registered length: 868ft 7in

Registered breadth: 97ft

Registered depth: 49ft 7in

Gross British: 45,649.99 tons

Sheer forward: 15ft

Sheer aft: 5ft 3in

Engine Particulars

Designed SHP: 60,000shp

Designed RPM: 180rpm

RPM on record voyage: 175.7rpm

Speed, designed: 23 knots

Speed, average: 23.6 knots

Draft leaving port – record voyage: 34ft 6in

Average slip percentage over ten voyages: 12.56 per cent

Average coal consumption

Per day – main engines only: 845.96 tons

Per day – auxiliaries only: 50 tons

Per day – all purposes: 900 tons

Per knot – record voyage: 1.5 tons/knot/hour

Per IHP per hour main engines: 1.26lb

Per SHP per hour main engines: 1.4lb

Per knot (tons): 1.48 tons/knot/hour

Propeller Particulars

Diameter: 16ft 6in

Pitch: 15ft 3in (average 15ft 5in – varying, from 1936)

Area of blades: 103sq.ft (125sq.ft from 1936)

Projected area: 90.6sq.ft

No. of blades on each propeller: 4

Built or solid: solid

Leonard Peskett's Recommendations

Leonard Peskett's report of *Aquitania*'s second round trip made a number of observations. He made a number of recommendations to improve the ship's accommodation:

1. Steam heaters to be fitted in bathrooms.
2. Supply a few small electric heaters for use in staterooms; portable lamp sockets (already fitted) to be used for these heaters. This will save putting steam on a section when heat is required by an individual passenger.
3. Consider fitting awnings to second- and third-class open promenades aft. When the wind is ahead, passengers are inconvenienced by fine ashes falling from the funnels.
4. Rooms in front of bridge house are let as outside rooms; at night time the covers to the ports of these rooms are closed, as the lights interferes with the navigation. The closing of the ports is a cause of dissatisfaction, and the fitting of outside jalousies might be considered.
5. Mats to be fitted on navigating bridge to prevent annoyance to passengers under.
6. Passenger lifts to be overhauled by the makers.
7. Sparred seats in third class to be fitted with stronger frames, and to have centre supports.
8. Third class covered promenades to be fitted with additional tables and chairs.
9. Mahogany rails and balusters to be fitted to interchangeable second- and third-class stairways.
10. Folding chairs (without footrests) to be supplied for the use of women in the third class. Chairs for women only to be placed outside second-class accommodation on C-deck.
11. A number of scuppers to be fitted on A-deck.
12. Exhaust fan to be fitted over the top of boat deck pantry.
13. Upper side panes of sliding windows (in first-class dining saloon) to be taken out for ventilation.
14. Cowls to Thermotank supplies to be removed, and covers to be fitted as per plan.
15. Air exhausts in first-class saloon to be fitted with baffles. Air supplies to be fitted with baffles where necessary.
16. Windows to be fitted to deck pantry doors where they are adjacent lift doors.
17. Shelves to be fitted in bathroom B98.
18. All brass covering plates over expansion joints to have 9in hinged piece in way of scuppers.
19. Expansion joints in air trucks C-deck to be completed.
20. Third-class stairways, treads to be altered, and where the stairs are steep, the number of treads to be reduced by one to give increased width of step. Brass nosings to be dispensed with.
21. There is a demand for more rooms for additional electricians and petty officers. It is submitted that extra rooms be provided on E-deck in positions marked on Plan.

Leonard Peskett, Cunard's naval architect. He oversaw *Aquitania*'s design, observing Cunard's little-known decision to remove the Turkish Baths in May 1912. In October 1912, Cunard decided to retain the swimming pool rather than replace it with a Turkish Bath establishment – against Mewès & Davis' recommendation. (*The Shipbuilder*, 1914/author's collection)

Facts and Figures of Thirty-Six Years

By the time *Aquitania* was withdrawn, her service record had surpassed many liners. Between 1920 and 1939, *Aquitania* carried a total of 293,931 passengers on westbound crossings and 236,818 passengers on eastbound crossings, making a total of 582 crossings. In service for longer than any of her rivals, in these years alone she carried more civilian passengers than (from the lowest to the highest) *Mauretania*, *Leviathan*, *Olympic*, *Majestic*, and *Berengaria*. Westbound, *Aquitania*'s passenger lists averaged 1,010 passengers over these nineteen years, while her eastbound crossings recorded passenger lists averaging 814 passengers. Any passengers carried on cruises do not appear to be included.

What of her war service? One set of Cunard figures show she steamed over 250,000 miles during the First World War, carrying over 145,000 'passengers' (i.e. service personnel), and that she steamed 526,264 miles during the Second World War, carrying no fewer than 384,596 'passengers.' There are minor variations with other figures, yet there is an apparent total of 529,596 military 'passengers'.

Aquitania appears to have carried a total of 1,200,000 'passengers' – including military personnel. In some cases the distinction between service personnel and civilian passengers is blurred, while the same is true for berths booked by Cunard and emigrants in the late 1940s. These appear to make finding specific, accurate figures next to impossible. One document lists *Aquitania* as carrying 135,000 'passengers' during the First World War; 530,749 passengers between the wars; and 384,586 'passengers' between November 1939 and the last day of 1945; and a figure of 128,691 passengers for the period from 1946, for a total of 1,179,026. The 11,208 passengers *Aquitania* carried in 1914 are wrongly included in the figure for post-1946, no passengers are listed for 1919, and the figures for the war years also vary slightly from other documents. (One otherwise accurate summary of the ship's life and technical statistics gave a total of 1,198,000 passengers.)

The figures for the final four years of *Aquitania*'s life are most problematic: 128,691 passengers sounds reasonable at first glance, yet it should be 117,483 since the document lists the totals for 1914, 1946, 1947, 1948 and 1949 and mistakenly adds them all up. In that the figures appear remarkably close to the North Atlantic Conference records, they presumably include berths booked by Cunard in the late 1940s and not emigrants or service personnel:

–	Westbound	Eastbound	Total
1946 ('to August')	25,960	21,375	47,335
1947	8,904	2,151	11,055
1948	19,763	8,110	27,873
1949	22,453	8,767	31,220

It is the distinction between passengers that blurs figures for 1946–49. One voyage-by-voyage list for 1946 gives 78,749 people carried on twenty-nine crossings, for an average of 2,715; and another for 1947 lists 93,794 people on thirty-five crossings at an average of 2,680. The figures are so high that it is probable they include all types of passenger and crew. Matching the total figures for 1946–47, one document gave the total for 1948–49 at 150,000, which seems a little high considering the smaller number of crossings.

Bearing in mind the confusion, perhaps the only reliable figures for 1946–49 are for those which seem to be limited to the berths sold directly by Cunard: totalling 117,483.

The confusion extended to Cunard officials as they tried to compile a list. One letter, dated 21 December 1949, stated that, 'the total movement in civilians, east and westbound from June 1945, to November 1949, between Britain and Canada, totals 103,486, which added to 989,550 makes the total commercial passengers carried by the ship 1,093,036.' Although the figure of 103,486 included some months in 1945, unfortunately it differs with the other figure of 117,483. How many civilian and service personnel, then, did *Aquitania* carry as passengers during her life? The short answer is 'a lot'!

Most estimates agree that *Aquitania* steamed around three million miles during her thirty-six years in service. The figure of 2,683,000 miles given by Cunard to the end of 1945 seems very specific, and would fit in with an eventual total of around three million miles.

Express Service Profits 1926–30

By means of comparison, this table includes the profits recorded by all three of Cunard's express ships from 1926 to 1930. These figures are apparently 'gross profits', with the ships' total disbursements being subtracted from the total earnings without account for such things as depreciation. *Aquitania*'s profits can be compared to those of her running mates: Cunard's gross profit of £1,858,247 in 1929 for their three ships compared favourably with the White Star Line's three express ships, which made a profit of £1,369,656 in 1929. The decline in profits in 1930 – the first year of the Depression – is evident:

Year	1926	1927	1928	1929	1930
Mauretania	£183,903	£223,650	£260,566	£391,580	£220,200
Aquitania	£488,438	£746,044	£708,516	£662,641	£550,604
Berengaria	£627,788	£554,647	£786,141	£804,026	£312,783

APPENDIX FIVE

RMS *Aquitania* Passenger Statistics

While *Aquitania* enjoyed an excellent reputation and was renowned for her popularity, it is in statistics that we can more easily quantify her success, from her surging passenger numbers in the early 1920s, the ongoing success until the decline of the early 1930s, and then the sharp recovery from 1934 even as she faced increasingly fierce competition. As *Aquitania* carried 530,749 passengers between the two wars, these figures work out to an average passenger list of 912 on her 582 crossings, clearly indicating a sustained level of popularity.

Aquitania's popularity compares well with her competitors, although her longevity helps skew comparisons. When ships such as the *Majestic* and *Leviathan* entered service after the war, they missed out on some of the early 1920s boom in passenger traffic, and since they were withdrawn from passenger service in the mid-1930s they did not really benefit from the recovery from the Depression. In contrast, *Aquitania*'s hectic schedule in the late 1930s

benefited her passenger-carrying statistics, even if passenger levels were still below those in the 1920s. Between 1920 and 1929, *Mauretania* carried 160,499 passengers with an average passenger list of 802; *Olympic* carried 264,265 passengers at an average of 951; *Aquitania* carried 306,914 passengers at an average of 1,171; and *Majestic* carried 274,514 passengers at an average of 1,248 per crossing from 1922–29.

The figures presented here are from the North Atlantic Conference's yearly tables from 1921 through to 1938. For some years, the number of round trips shown may differ from other sources due to rounding.

Year	Round trips	Passengers carried	Average per crossing
1921	15	60,587	2,019
1922	15	41,000	1,367

Year	Round trips	Passengers carried	Average per crossing	Year	Round trips	Passengers carried	Average per crossing
1923	13½	29,230	1,082	1931	18	21,992	611
1924	15	32,303	1,077	1932	11	14,435	656
1925	14½	28,215	973	1933	15	13,922	464
1926	13	26,220	1,008	1934	13½	13,317	493
1927	16½	31,963	940	1935	14	16,022	572
1928	14½	28,033	967	1936	17	21,683	638
1929	14	29,363	1,049	1937	18	26,389	733
1930	16	27,895	872	1938	13½	18,644	691

APPENDIX SIX

Cunard and White Star's Express Service Passenger Carryings

As the 1920s came to a close and the Depression began to bite in 1930, both Cunard and White Star's express liners suffered. This is perhaps best shown by the total number of passengers carried by *Aquitania*, *Berengaria* and *Mauretania*, and *Homeric*, *Majestic* and *Olympic* on the Atlantic run. Cruise passengers are not included, although that was the primary employment for *Homeric* and *Mauretania* by 1932–33.

Year	1927	1928	1929	1930	1931	1932	1933
Cunard	86,983	82,017	85,058	67,173	47,960	43,262	30,918
White Star	76,328	77,242	74,506	60,657	36,217	28,946	22,702

APPENDIX SEVEN

RMS *Aquitania*'s Voyages 329–374

Aquitania's life during the Second World War is recorded in detail in surviving Cunard documents. They show her as she travelled around the globe – far outside the Atlantic service that she was designed for – while being driven hard even as she surpassed thirty years' service:

Voyage number	Date	Itinerary
329	29 November 1939–21 December 1939	Southampton, Halifax, Gourock, Southampton.
330	16 January 1940–14 February 1940	Southampton, Halifax, Gourock, Southampton.

Voyage number	Date	Itinerary
331	9 March 1940–20 April 1940	Southampton, Freetown, Cape Town, Fremantle, Sydney, Wellington.
332	2 May 1940–22 June 1940	Wellington, Fremantle, Cape Town, Simonstown, Freetown, Greenock, Liverpool.
333	29 June 1940–29 July 1940	Liverpool, Freetown, Cape Town, Simonstown, Colombo.
334	3 August 1940–15 September 1940	Colombo, Fremantle, Sydney, Fremantle, Bombay.
335	22 September 1940–4 November 1940	Bombay, Fremantle, Sydney, Fremantle, Bombay.
336	8 November 1940–29 January 1941	Bombay, Fremantle, Sydney, Fremantle, Colombo, Fremantle, Sydney.
337	8 February 1941–17 March 1941	Sydney, Fremantle, Bombay, Singapore (dry dock).
338	26 April 1941–15 June 1941	Singapore, Colombo, Suez, Trincomalee, Fremantle, Sydney.
339	22 June 1941–23 August 1941	Sydney, Wellington, Fremantle, Trincomalee, Port Tewfik, Colombo, Fremantle, Sydney.
340	5 September 1941–28 November 1941	Sydney, Wellington, Fremantle, Colombo, Port Tewfik, Bombay, Colombo, Singapore, Sydney.
341	28 December 1941–8 January 1942	Sydney, Port Moresby, Sydney.
342	10 January 1942–31 January 1942	Sydney, Fremantle, Ratui Bay, Fremantle, Sydney.
343	10 February 1942–1 March 1942	Sydney, Honolulu, San Francisco.
344	10 March 1942–24 March 1942	San Francisco, Honolulu, San Francisco.
345	30 March 1942–23 April 1942	San Francisco, Honolulu, San Pedro, Panama, New York.
346	30 April 1942–12 May 1942	New York, Clyde.
347	31 May 1942–14 August 1942	Clyde, Freetown, Simonstown, Diego Suarez, Aden, Suez, Diego Suarez, Cape Town, Freetown, Boston.
348	6 September 1942–27 November 1942	Boston, New York, Rio de Janeiro, Cape Town, Aden, Suez, Aden, Fremantle, Wellington.
349	12 December 1942–26 February 1943	Wellington, Fremantle, Port Tewfik, Massawa, Port Tewfik, Massawa, HM Base East Indies, Fremantle, Sydney.
350	23 March 1943–31 May 1943	Sydney, Fremantle, Cape Town, Rio de Janeiro, New York, Clyde.
351	31 May 1943–15 July 1943	Clyde, New York (dry dock), Clyde.
352	21 July 1943–11 August 1943	Clyde, New York, Clyde.
353	16 August 1943–9 October 1943	Clyde, New York, Clyde.
354	12 October 1943–29 October 1943	Clyde, New York, Clyde.
355–62	4 November 1943–29 June 1944	Clyde, New York, Clyde.
363–74	3 July 1944–16 May 1945	North Atlantic voyages – Clyde-Halifax (4), Clyde – New York (8).

Aquitania is visible in the background in this view of Port Said, *c.*1932. (Author's collection, courtesy Eric Longo and Timothy Trower)

RMS *Aquitania*'s Captains

It is inevitable that any liner will have a number of commanders during her life. Apparently published for the first time, this is a comprehensive list of *Aquitania*'s captains, giving their name, age, number and the dates that they first signed on (where recorded).

Although every effort has been made to be accurate, there are some contradictions even in primary sources like crew agreements and the ship's log. To avoid duplication, rather than give the dates that every captain signed on again for subsequent voyages, only the date that the captain's successor signed on is given. Ages are given where known, for when each captain signed on initially, and every effort has been made to spell names correctly and cross-reference material, yet faded and smudged names can introduce errors. At times, especially during the 1940s, captains changed frequently, and this makes compiling any list doubly difficult.

Name	Age	Certificate Number	Date
Captain William J. Turner	57	021687	30 May 1914
Captain Ernest R. Loring	–	–	7 August 1914
Captain D. Dow	55	–	19 May 1915
Captain Charles A. Smith	51	012114	24 June 1915
Captain John T.W. Charles	53	015759	23 January 1918
Captain E.T. Britten	51	031493	13 August 1926
Captain John T.W. Charles	–	015759	31 August 1926
Captain A. Rostron	56	022747	26 January 1927
Captain John T.W. Charles	–	015759	11 February 1927
Captain S.G.S. McNeil	54	02237	–
Captain John T.W. Charles	–	015759	–
Captain A.C. Greig	47	035396	9 April 1927
Captain John T.W. Charles	–	015759	26 April 1927
Captain A. Rostron	56	022747	2 November 1927
Captain John T.W. Charles	–	015759	23 November 1927
Captain E. G. Diggle	56	025938	28 March 1928
Captain John T.W. Charles	–	015759	27 June 1928
Captain Guy R. Dolphin	48	003254	15 July 1928
Captain E.G. Diggle	–	025938	8 August 1928
Captain William Prothero	56	025281	23 November 1928
Captain E.G. Diggle	–	025938	12 December 1928
Captain William Prothero	–	025281	23 January 1929
Captain E.G. Diggle	–	025938	8 February 1929
Captain William Prothero	–	025281	5 April 1929
Captain E.G. Diggle	–	025938	27 April 1929
Captain William Prothero	–	025281	10 August 1929
Captain E.G. Diggle	–	025938	31 August 1929

Name	Age	Certificate Number	Date
Captain William Prothero	–	025281	26 April 1930
Captain E.G. Diggle	–	025938	3 June 1930
Captain William Prothero	–	025281	30 August 1930
Captain William Prothero	–	025281	16 September 1930
Captain E.G. Diggle	–	025938	20 September 1930
Captain R.B. Irving	54	002045	7 August 1931
Captain J.C. Townley	52	034482	15 June 1932
Captain R.B. Irving	–	002045	8 July 1932
Captain J.C. Townley	–	034482	7 September 1932
Captain R.B. Irving	–	002045	28 September 1932
Captain George Gibbons	53	036447	8 March 1933
Captain R.B. Irving	–	002045	28 March 1933
Captain George Gibbons	–	036447	2 June 1933
Captain R.B. Irving	–	002045	23 June 1933
Captain J.C. Townley	–	034482	18 April 1934
Captain George Gibbons	–	036447	6 July 1934
Captain P.R. Vaughan	58	030781	21 January 1935
Captain George Gibbons	–	036447	17 April 1935
Captain P.R. Vaughan	58	030781	7 May 1935
Captain R.V. Peel	59	031038	14 June 1935
Captain George Gibbons	–	036447	18 September 1935
Captain R.V. Peel	–	031038	9 October 1935
Captain R.B. Irving	–	002045	31 December 1935
Captain A.T. Brown	53	035106	4 November 1936
Captain R.B. Irving	–	002045	16 December 1936
Captain Guy R. Dolphin	58	003254	24 August 1937
Captain J.C. Townley	–	034482	4 October 1937
Captain E. Edkin	57	035796	30 November 1937
Captain J.C. Townley	–	034482	3 January 1938
Captain George Gibbons	–	036447	13 April 1938
Captain Goldley	–		25 May 1938
Captain George Gibbons	–	036447	6 July 1938
Captain J.C. Townley	–	034482	27 July 1938
Captain George Gibbons	–	036447	21 July 1939
Captain G. Bate	58	035048	20 November 1939
Captain George Gibbons	–	036447	29 November 1939
Captain Andrew MacDonald	59	037036	15 February 1940
Captain J.D. Snow	–	039070	2 March 1940
Captain George Gibbons	–	036447	2 March 1940

Name	Age	Certificate Number	Date
Captain J.D. Snow	–	039070	19 December 1941
Captain E.M. Fall	59	038956	4 March 1942
Captain Walter C. Battle	60	001986	24 April 1942
Captain C.M. Ford	55	004621	12 May 1943
Captain Walter C. Battle	–	001986	20 May 1943
Captain C.M. Ford	–	004621	30 May 1943
Captain B. Aston	–		1 November 1943
Captain C.M. Ford	–	004621	18 December 1943
Captain Walter C. Battle	–	001986	29 February 1944
Captain C.M. Ford	–	004621	1 March 1944
Captain C.G. Illingworth	59	039271	25 March 1944
Captain R. Spencer	–	041186	25 March 1944
Captain Walter C. Battle	–	001986	4 June 1944
Captain C.G. Illingworth	59	039271	16 June 1944
Captain E.M. Fall	–	038956	27 June 1944
Captain Walter C. Battle	–	001986	11 August 1944
Captain E.M. Fall	–	038956	15 August 1944
Captain D. Smythe	–	–	5 September 1944
Captain Walter C. Battle	–	001986	23 November 1944
Captain Walter C. Battle	–	001986	29 December 1944
Captain E.M. Fall	–	038956	3 January 1945
Captain C.M. Ford	–	004621	21 January 1945
Captain G.E. Cove	–	041348	21 January 1945
Captain H.G. Norris	–	–	2 February 1945
Captain R. Spencer	–	041186	6 February 1945
Captain E.M. Fall	–	038956	21 May 1945
Captain C.M. Ford	–	004621	18 June 1945
Captain J.D. Snow	–	039070	4 September 1945
Captain Andrew MacDonald	–	004212	28 May 1946
Captain J.D. Jones	–	–	17 June 1946
Captain J.D. Snow	–	039070	9 July 1946
Captain G.E. Cove	–	041348	6 August 1946
Captain G.E. Cove	–	041348	22 October 1946
Captain J.D. Snow	–	039070	22 October 1946
Captain G.E. Cove	–	041348	11 December 1946
Captain J.D. Snow	–	039070	18 January 1947
Captain G.E. Cove	–	041348	8 March 1947
Captain J.D. Snow	–	039070	20 June 1947
Captain G.E. Cove	–	041348	7 July 1947
Captain Andrew MacDonald	–	004212	10 October 1947
Captain G.E. Cove	–	041348	11 December 1947
Captain H. Grattidge	–	008257	4 February 1948
Captain R.B.G. Woollatt	–	041860	11 June 1948
Captain G.E. Cove	–	041348	2 July 1948

Name	Age	Certificate Number	Date
Captain H. Grattidge	–	008257	2 July 1948
Captain R.B.G. Woollatt	–	041860	2 July 1948
Captain G.E. Cove	–	041348	5 July 1948
Captain H. Grattidge	–	008257	23 July 1948
Captain R.G. Thelwell	–	0012875	23 July 1948
Captain R.B.G. Woollatt	–	041860	13 August 1948
Captain H. Grattidge	–	008257	14 August 1948
Captain D.M. MacLaren	–	–	14 August 1948
Captain R.B.G. Woollatt	–	041860	14 October 1948
Captain R.G. Thelwell	–	0012875	26 November 1948
Captain R.B.G. Woollatt	–	041860	6 January 1949
Captain R.G. Thelwell	–	0012875	6 January 1949
Captain R.B.G. Woollatt	–	041860	26 March 1949
Captain R.G. Thelwell	–	0012875	14 June 1949
Captain R.B.G. Woollatt	–	041860	22 June 1949
Captain R.G. Thelwell	–	0012875	20 August 1949
Captain R.B.G. Woollatt	–	041860	20 August 1949
Captain R.G. Thelwell	–	0012875	25 August 1949
Captain R.B.G. Woollatt	–	041860	10 September 1949
Captain A. MacKellar	52	0014734	6 December 1949
Captain R.B.G. Woollatt	–	041860	18 February 1950

Among some of the ship's log books and crew agreements, one document entitled 'Detail of Masters 1943–49' summarised *Aquitania*'s commanders. While it differs from other documents, it gives the commanders as follows: Captain T.B. Mardox, aged 59, certificate 022865, from 27 October 1943 to 4 November 1943; Captain C.M. Ford, aged 56, certificate 004621, from 4 November 1943 to 26 November 1943; Captain R.B.G. Woollatt, aged 57, certificate 041860, from 26 November 1943 to 21 December 1943; Captain C.M. Ford, from 21 December 1943 to 24 March 1944; Captain C.G. Illingworth, aged 59, certificate 039271, 24 March 1944 to 1 July 1944; Captain E.M. Fall, aged 61, certificate 038926, from 1 July 1944 to 5 September 1944; Captain R. Spencer, aged 55, certificate 041186, 5 September 1944 to 6 October 1944; Captain W.C. Battle, aged 63, certificate 001986, 7 October 1944 to 4 February 1945; Captain E.M. Fall, from 4 February 1945 to 18 June 1945; Captain G.E. Cove, aged 56, certificate 041348, from 20 June 1945 to 14 October 1945; Captain C.M. Ford, from 25 October 1945 to 11 January 1946; Captain J.D. Snow, aged 56, certificate 039070, from 26 January 1946 to 10 May 1946; Captain J.C. MacDonald, aged 60, certificate 004212, from 14 May 1946 to 6 August 1946; Captain R.G. Thelwell, aged 49, certificate 0012875 (no date); Captain J.D. Snow, 9 August 1946 to 8 March 1947; Captain G.E. Cove, 10 March 1947 to 11 December 1947; Captain J.D. Snow, 15 December 1947 to 3 January 1948; Captain G.E. Cove, from 4 January 1948 to 8 April 1949; Captain J.C. MacDonald, 8 April 1948 to 20 May 1948; Captain G.E. Cove, from 22 May 1948 to 22 July 1948; Captain H. Grattidge, certificate 008257, from 27 July 1948 to 4 November 1948; Captain R.B.G. Woollatt, from 9 November 1948 to 24 March 1949; Captain R.G. Thelwall, from 25 March 1949 to 14 April 1949; Captain R.B.G. Woollatt, from 15 April 1949 to 24 August 1949; Captain R.G. Thelwall, from 24 August 1949 to 29 September 1949; Captain R.B.G. Woollatt, from 30 September 1949 to 9 December 1949.

BIBLIOGRAPHY

Published Sources

Braynard, Frank. *Leviathan* Volume 5. 1981.

Britten, Sir Edgar T. *A Million Ocean Miles*. Hutchinson & Co. Ltd. 1936.

Hutchings, David F. *RMS* Queen Elizabeth: *From Victory to Valhalla*. Kingfisher Publications; 1990.

Hood, A.G. (Ed.) *The* Aquitania. *Souvenir Number of* The Shipbuilder, Special Number: Midsummer 1914.

McCart, Neil. *Atlantic Liners of the Cunard Line: From 1884 to the Present Day*. Patrick Stephens Ltd. 1990.

McCart, Neil. *SS* Aquitania: *Cunard's Atlantic Liner*. Fan Publications. 1994.

Morton, Leslie. *The Long Wake*. Routledge & Keegan Paul Ltd. 1968.

Priestley, J. B. *Midnight on the Desert*. Heinemann. 1937.

Satchell, Alister. *Running the Gauntlet: How Three Great Liners Carried A Million Men To War, 1942–45*. Chatham Publishing; 2001.

Spedding, Charles T. *Reminiscences of Transatlantic Travellers*. T. Fisher Unwin. 1926.

Streater, L., & Streater, R.A. Aquitania: *Cunard's Greatest Dream*. The Maritime Publishing Co. 1997.

Warren, Mark D. (Ed.) *The Quadruple-Screw Turbine-Driven Cunard Liner* Aquitania. (Reprinted from Engineering). Patrick Stephens Ltd, 1988.

Warren, Mark D. *Shipbuilder* Volume 2: 1907–14. Blue Riband Publications. 1997.

Williamson, Ellen. *When We Went First Class*. Doubleday Garden City: 1977.

Archival Sources

Glasgow University Archive Services

USC1/101/71.

National Archives (The Public Records Office)

ADM 1/10407; ADM 1/16773; ADM 53/33908; ADM 137/3423; BT 100/502–73; BT380/1113–36; MT 15/428; MT 15/505; MT 15/522; MT 15/702; MT 15/830; MT 23/591; MT 23/596; MT23/637; MT 23/781; MT 25/9; MT 73/51.

National Museums Liverpool (Maritime Archives & Library, Merseyside Maritime Museum)

B/CUN/3/5/1; B/CUN/3/8/7; B/CUN/3/14/1; B/CUN/4/4/5; B/CUN/4/8/9.

The Cunard Archive, Sydney Jones Library, Liverpool University

AC14/7; AC14/88; AC14/199/3; B1/9; B2; B2/1; B6/7; D922/3/1/3; D922/3/1/23; GM 3/2–3; GM 8/1/26–32; GM 12/5 & 6; PR3/19/42; PR5/2; PR3/9/11a; PR3.12/41; PR5/24/33; S/7/3/5.

'I feel I cannot let today pass without expressing through you my sadness at this final parting with the *Aquitania*. In peace and war, fair weather and foul, she has done her duty in a manner unsurpassed by any other of her sisters who have helped to build up the company's long history. With all truth can it be said "She did well to the end," and that must be the thought of all who have sailed in, or served with, her in our fleet.' – Signal from the chairman of the Cunard Steamship Company Limited, Mr. F.A. Bates, MC, AFC, DL, to Captain R.B.G. Woollatt, RD, RNR, commanding *Aquitania* on the Occasion of the Hauling Down of the Cunard Flag, 18 February 1950.

'On behalf of myself, officers and ship's company I thank you for your kind message of February 18th. All aboard feel both sadness at parting with the *Aquitania* and pride in the achievements of a great ship, sentiments which they are privileged to share with you, the management and staff both ashore and afloat.' – Reply to the chairman from Captain Woollatt.

S.S. 'AQUITANIA' IN HEAVY SEA. N<u>o</u>2. SEPT: 1930.

'The time may arrive in the passing of the centuries when the art of shipbuilding will have become forgotten. Our descendents may wonder, as we today marvel at the pyramids, how men could possibly launch – let alone build – such a mammoth vessel as the *Aquitania*. Perhaps somewhere in a library or museum, there may hereafter be preserved a picture of this ship with some details as to her size. And they will ask themselves how mere human beings of flesh and blood could create such a wonder of engineering...' – E. Keble Chatterton, 1913.

If you are interested in purchasing other books published by The History Press, or in case
you have difficulty finding any books in your local bookshop, you can also place orders
directly through our website
www.thehistorypress.co.uk